Word Problems

Grades 6-8

By
Harold Torrance

Cover Illustration by
Jeff Van Kanegan

Published by Instructional Fair • TS Denison
an imprint of

 McGraw Hill **Children's Publishing**

Author: Harold Torrance
Cover Illustration: Jeff Van Kanegan
Photo Credits: Stockbyte
Inside Illustrations: Randy Rider

 Children's Publishing

Published by Instructional Fair • TS Denison
An imprint of McGraw-Hill Children's Publishing
Copyright © 2001 McGraw-Hill Children's Publishing

Send all inquiries to:
McGraw-Hill Children's Publishing
3195 Wilson Drive NW
Grand Rapids, Michigan 49544

Word Problems—grades 6–8
ISBN: 0-7424-0136-7

3 4 5 6 7 8 9 PHXBK 08 07 06 05 04 03

The *McGraw-Hill* Companies

Introduction

Word problems have long been a source of confusion for students. Figuring out ways to teach students how to solve them has been a source of frustration for teachers as well. A student typically looks at a page of word problems with very little enthusiasm. Often a mix of fear and anger is associated with word problem activities. To make matters worse, these attitudes may have been present before students were even assigned to your class. These perceptions *can* affect the student's capacity to deal with word problems, perhaps even more than the lack of necessary computational skills.

The problems in this book are very long by the usual standards. They are written in the style of lengthy "story" problems on purpose. They describe situations encountered by people in business settings, in their homes, while working with hobbies, and in a multitude of other realistic settings. These settings will demonstrate to students the practical nature of word problems. The length also will force the student to slow down and actually *read* each problem.

Information is presented to the student in a narrative format. Sometimes the numbers needed for working a problem are revealed near the very beginning, sometimes near the end. Often other figures are thrown in, not for the sake of confusion, but to give the student the opportunity to discriminate useful information from irrelevant information.

The problems are designed to force a *new* pattern of behavior on the student. Students seem to have the notion that the words in a word problem are simply obstacles to their quickly gleaning the numbers out of the problem and doing a computation. For working word problems, speed is *not* what students need. These problems will slow them down a bit, forcing students to read and understand the problem before taking action to solve it. Once students know what the problem is about and understand what it is asking, they have probably cleared the biggest hurdle! By the time this book is finished, students ideally will have developed a new pattern of behavior for approaching word problems.

Table of Contents

Horse Buyer Does Homework

Sylvia wants a horse. She has decided that the best way to convince her parents to buy a horse is having all the facts involved and being ready to sensibly discuss the matter. That is why Sylvia is researching all matters related to horses. She plans to arm herself with information about the care and upkeep of horses, the equipment and supplies needed, and the costs involved.

Sylvia has found a place nearby that boards horses. She thinks that it would be an ideal place to keep a horse since a friend has recommended the facility and it is so close by. The owners of the boarding facility charge $95 per month to board a horse. How much can Sylvia tell her parents it would cost per year to keep a horse boarded at this facility? _____

Sylvia's parents did not take her horse idea very seriously at first. They told her that buying and keeping a horse would be too expensive. Sylvia stuck to the facts, though, and she was able to counter many of her parents' concerns. Her parents agreed that she could have a horse only if she could prove that she was able to pay for the horse and its proper upkeep. Sylvia's father finally said, "You come up with $2,500 to put into this idea and it is fine with me."

What her parents did not know was that Sylvia had been quietly saving her money for close to three years, gradually building up a horse fund. She had $1,670 stuffed in a cookie tin in her room. This was mostly money that she had received from doing chores around the house and from baby-sitting for neighbors. Some of the money came from birthday gifts. When Sylvia shared her secret with her grandmother, her grandmother offered to help with a contribution of $500 to the horse fund. How much money does Sylvia still need to complete her horse fund?

_____

Old House Needs Fixing

Mandy purchased a house in the historic district. The house is known as "Corner Stand." A previous owner named the house many years ago, and the name managed to stay with the house each time its ownership changed hands. Structurally the house is in fine condition. The exterior of the house has been maintained fairly well. It is the interior of the house that concerns Mandy. A number of things in the house need repairs, restoration, or replacement. Her budget is rather strict and allows her only $20,000 to make all the necessary repairs.

Three different heating companies have submitted bids for replacing the old heating system. She wants to have a heat pump installed to replace the oil furnace. A certain amount of work is also needed for cutting new vents and installing ducts to carry the heated air. Jiffy Heating & Air-Conditioning submitted a bid of $6,800. Trustworthy Contracting submitted a bid of $8,250. Air Systems turned in a bid of $5,995, but Mandy was not fully confident of their capability to do the work properly and did not further consider them for the job. How much more money will Mandy have available in her overall repair budget once the heating system work is completed if she chooses Jiffy Heating and Air-Conditioning instead of Trustworthy Contracting? _____

Mandy has noticed that the back patio is a bit weathered looking and will need repainting. The patio has dimensions of 12 feet by 18 feet. The paint she is buying is expensive and Mandy wants to buy only enough for the job. A quart of this paint costs $12.99 and will cover 90 square feet. If the paint she has selected for the porch is sold only by the quart, how much money will Mandy end up spending on paint for this job? _____

More About Mandy and Corner Stand

Mandy plans to refinish the wood floor in one of the rooms at Corner Stand. The previous owner told her that the room was used as an old-fashioned parlor for entertaining visitors. Over the years the floor received a heavy volume of foot traffic. The wood itself is worn down in spots, and there is an ugly coat of wax and old finish on other areas of the floor. For this project Mandy will need to thoroughly sand the entire area and apply two coats of clear finish to the floor.

Mandy is keeping a log of her time spent on this kind of work so that she will have some idea of the "sweat-equity" she has put into the house. She is certain that these kinds of improvements will add to the value of the house. Renting the equipment and purchasing the necessary supplies took her 1 hour, 20 minutes. Sanding the floor and removing the dust took her 6 hours, 22 minutes. Preparing the wood surface and applying the first finish coat took 2 hours, 47 minutes. The second finish coat took only 1 hour, 35 minutes to apply. Final cleanup and returning the rented equipment took 48 minutes. How much time did Mandy put into completing this project?

_____

Mandy's next project is selecting a piece of carpet for a small upstairs bedroom. The room measures 12 feet by 12 feet. (Mandy knows that carpet is sold by the square yard, so she will convert these figures to equivalent yards before making her area computations.) Mandy wants to buy a piece of carpet the exact size of the room so that it can be rolled out and will fit the available space exactly. She does not want the carpet installed, since she may later change her mind about the planned use for this room. How many square yards of carpet will Mandy be buying for this room?

_____

Time Bothers Debater

Drew is a prominent member on his school's debate team. Team members have come to count on Drew for a sure "place" at competitions. Often Drew will win individual events outright. Drew has been working on an oration. His speech is designed to be a persuasive argument concerning a current political topic. Drew has done this kind of activity before, but he is having trouble with the time limit for this speech.

The speech is supposed to take between 3 minutes, 45 seconds and 4 minutes to deliver. Penalties are imposed if a speech is shorter or longer. Drew knows that he has a tendency to speed through his material a bit at the actual debate competition, so he tries to practice his speech to last exactly 255 seconds during practice sessions. Currently Drew's speech is running only 3 minutes, 21 seconds in recent practice sessions. How many more seconds does Drew need to extend his speech to reach his target for the practice sessions? _____

In Drew's school district, debate teams are scored on a points system to determine the overall winner of a competition. First, second, and third place finishes in individual events are assigned points that contribute to a team's total. The competition lasts until a team wins 300 points. According to the rules, any team having less than 200 points at the close of the competition cannot be awarded second or third place.

At a recent event, Drew's team had earned 228 points when another team ended the competition by winning their 300th point. Drew's team was 44 points behind the second place winner. How many points behind the winning team was Drew's team? _____

Weather Project

Marty is doing a weather research project as part of a school assignment. She is monitoring both the temperature and precipitation for each day. In the morning at 7 a.m. she takes a temperature reading. She takes another temperature reading at 3 p.m. and also checks the rain gauge for any new precipitation at that time. At 9 p.m. Marty takes the last temperature reading for the day.

Marty will continue to take these readings until data for 60 consecutive days has been accumulated. She thinks that this is enough time to provide a body of data for her project. At the end of the 60 days, how many more readings will she have collected for temperature than for precipitation? _____

HOT STUFF!

Marty chose to use the Fahrenheit temperature scale over the Celsius scale. She thinks Fahrenheit figures are more readily understood by people. Since she will be rounding all temperature figures to the nearest whole number, Fahrenheit also provides a more precise measure for her temperature readings than Celsius.

Marty was quite surprised in looking at her temperature data to see that a span of 31 degrees had occurred between the 7 a.m. and the 3 p.m. readings on a single day. She found it somewhat incredible that the temperature could rise so much during such a short span. If the temperature was 43 degrees at 7 a.m. on this particular day, what was it at 3 p.m.? _____

Planning Goes into Photo Album

Charlotte has a number of loose pictures. She would like to organize the better ones into an album. Many of the pictures are from film she has shot herself, while a lot of the photographs were given to her. Charlotte first plans to sort the loose photos so she can get some idea of how many albums will be needed. With an afternoon of sorting behind her, she has managed to pare down 1,200 loose pictures into a stack of 132. The stack of 132 better photos are the ones she will put into albums; the rest will go back into a box.

Now that Charlotte knows how many photos she wants to display in an album, she can choose the album that best fits her needs. After much looking, she settled on an album costing $14.99. The album comes with 20 pages and additional pages can be added. Single pages may be purchased separately for $1.29 each. Charlotte liked this particular album because the pages will hold 3 photos on each side of a single page. How much will it cost Charlotte to put together an album capable of holding the 132 photos she wants displayed? _____

After sorting all those photos, Charlotte decided that she needed a new digital camera. That would allow her to view the photos on her computer monitor and save or print out only the ones she wants. Charlotte figures that it beats sorting boxes of photos or paying for expensive albums.

The camera shop where Charlotte buys all her photography equipment has a digital camera she likes. The model has a zoom lens and built-in flash. It normally sells for $579, but the shop is currently running a sale on it for $529. The shop will even take Charlotte's old camera as a trade-in at $45, since they also sell used camera equipment. How much will it cost Charlotte to get the new digital camera if she uses her old camera as a trade-in?

_____

More About Charlotte and Her Photography

Charlotte has been experimenting with her new digital camera. She is still trying to get used to the new features. One habit that Charlotte cannot seem to break is her reluctance to actually take pictures. With her old camera a 36-exposure roll of film cost $5.52, and having it developed was usually $15. The new camera essentially costs nothing to take a picture because the picture is stored in the camera's memory and deleted if it is not wanted. No more film to buy!

Charlotte is trying to get used to the notion that taking pictures really costs her nothing and that she is now free to experiment with her shots. How much did it previously cost Charlotte on average, per picture, to shoot a 36-exposure roll of film in her old camera, including the developing charges? _____

Charlotte has found one big drawback with her new digital camera. The camera runs on four AA-size batteries, and it will drain them completely in just one or two afternoons of usage. Charlotte noticed that using the zoom lens, a mechanically driven portion of the camera, seems to speed up the battery drain.

Charlotte pays $3.69 for a pack of four AA batteries where she shops. She has been buying a lot of these batteries lately but thinks they are quite cheap compared to the cost of film and processing with her old camera. If Charlotte has already used 28 AA batteries with her new digital camera, how much has she spent on batteries? _____

Boat Show No Bargain

Henry and Josh are planning to attend a boat show. The show is being held at Exhibit Hall, next to the sports stadium. It has been advertised as the "largest boat extravaganza ever." Josh has heard that over 500 boats plus hundreds of marine equipment dealers will be crammed into Exhibit Hall.

Henry has agreed to pay all expenses related to their attending the boat show since Josh paid the last time the two went out to eat. Henry and Josh considered taking the transit system since it has a stop quite near Exhibit Hall, but they decided at the last minute to go in Henry's car. Parking in the multi-level garage at the Hall costs $12 per vehicle. Optional valet parking was an extra $3.50. Admission to the boat show was $9.50 per person. Josh did have a $2.50 discount coupon, but it only applied to the admission for one admission ticket. How much did Henry spend to get them parked and into the boat show if he chose not to use the valet parking but did use Josh's coupon? _____

Henry does not have a boat, but he likes the nautical style of clothing that boating enthusiasts wear. One of the dealers had a number of racks of clothes designed for sailing under adverse conditions. Henry thought the rainproof garments would work well for his job as an outdoor landscaper. He has never quite found a good rain outfit that works while planting shrubs, spreading gravel, etc.

Henry selected a jacket with a rain hood at a cost of $249.95. Henry also chose the matching pants for this outfit at a cost of $119.95. The clothing dealer offered to give Henry a knit cap with a retail value of $16.95 and a pair of socks with a retail value of $12.95 since he was buying a complete outfit. Josh thinks Henry has lost his mind since most of their work clothes would not cost $50 if added up from head to toe. How much money is Henry spending on his new rainproof outfit?

_____

More About the Boat Show

Henry and Josh may have found a boat at the show. At times, the two have talked about splitting the cost of a fishing boat. The idea of spending sunny days out on the open water fishing for their favorite game fish has both of them quite excited. Normally, the city pier is as close to the water as the two get for their fishing outings.

The boat being considered by Henry and Josh is a 14-foot TroutMaster Deluxe. The salesman told them that this boat is rated for a 200-horsepower motor that will produce speeds of up to 50 miles per hour in calm water conditions. After finding out Henry and Josh's maximum boat budget, the salesman suggested a 15-horsepower motor. Monthly payments on a boat properly configured for Henry and Josh's true needs will cost $319.50 per month for 4 years. If Henry and Josh buy the TroutMaster Deluxe and agree to split monthly payments equally, how much will the boat payments alone have cost each of them by the time this boat is paid for? _____

When Henry called his wife from the boat show to run the boat idea by her before signing the contract, she told him not to bother coming home if he bought the boat. Henry took this to mean that there was very little flexibility in her position on the matter. Josh also met with the same resistance from his wife.

Henry and Josh were still excited about boats and fishing, so the two bought tickets with a charter service that runs daily fishing trips. The charter service charges $49.50 per person for a day-long fishing trip, which includes all bait and equipment needed. Drinks and a boxed lunch are optional at a cost of $8.50 per person. The charter

service also sells embroidered fishing caps at a cost of $15 each. Henry and Josh have decided to go "all out" on this trip. The two feel like they deserve it since they could not buy their own boat. How much will the chartered fishing trip cost each of them including the boxed lunch and embroidered fishing cap? _____

Airplane Not Unlike Automobile

The engine in Carolyn's airplane is serviced on a schedule based on the number of hours it has operated. Every 100 hours, the plane must go in for regular maintenance and inspections. Carolyn has been looking at her flight log. She has had a number of flights since the last engine service. The following flights, listed in terms of hours, are noted in her flight log: 3.5, 2.25, 7.0, 6.75, 4.5, 5.0, 9.25, 1.5, 2.5, 3.0. How many more hours can the plane be operated before the regular engine service is due?

_____

Carolyn has just agreed to test drive a new battery-operated car. One of her friends, an employee of a large automobile manufacturer, has arranged for the test. Carolyn will use this car for a one-week period, keeping entries on how well the car performs and any changes she might suggest for the car's design.

LET'S GO!

The new electric car is made of lighter-than-normal materials to extend battery life. Rechargeable batteries provide the main source of power for this car, but unlike many other electric car designs, a small gasoline motor will operate this car when the batteries are dead. When fully charged, the batteries will power this car for 5 hours at a top speed of 50 miles per hour. The gasoline motor will then run the car for 2 hours at a speed of 50 miles per hour. What is the maximum distance the car could be driven by first using the batteries, and then the gasoline engine at the suggested speed of 50 mph?

_____

Art Museum Provides Inspiration

Henry and Josh recently attended a special exhibit of famous impressionists at the art museum. It was not their idea. Both of their wives wanted to see the exhibit, and the two were forced to attend. Henry thought that the impressionist art looked like a bunch of blurry but colorful paintings done by children. Josh was convinced that he could do as well himself at home.

Josh did find cause for inspiration at the museum. Since Josh works in construction and he occasionally assists with plumbing projects at work, he found the museum's sensor-operated sinks and toilets to be works of art in their own right. Josh was lucky enough to bump into the museum's maintenance director, and the two began talking about the sensor-operated sinks. The maintenance director told Josh that the six sensor-operated sinks in the men's rest room were new. They each saved an average of 275 gallons of water each month over the old sinks. How many total gallons of water does this bank of sensor-operated sinks in the men's room save the museum each month? _____

Henry also found something inspiring at the museum. A pen in the gift shop had a rendition of a famous painting depicted in the barrel of the pen. The painting showed

BUT IS IT ART?

a brilliant yellow grain field that appeared to have recently been harvested. A large flock of black crows were depicted flying over the field. By tilting the pen upside down the birds would magically pass over the field. The painting appeared as normal when the pen was held upright as it would be used for writing. Henry thought this was really neat and he bought a pen for himself, another as a gift for Josh, and four more for the guys he works with. The pens cost $2.39 each. Sales tax was $.16 on each pen. How much money did Henry spend on these art pens?

_____

Miles Per Gallon Mean Money

Annie has been transferred to the transportation division of her company. The company's president told Annie that her top priority in the new job will be finding ways for the company to save money on its transportation expenses. Annie already has some ideas. She knows that the Miles Per Gallon (MPG) rating of company vehicles will be an important figure to evaluate. The number of miles a vehicle can travel on a single gallon of gasoline largely determines how much it will cost to operate that vehicle.

Annie has asked one of the delivery van drivers to participate in a test. He will fill the gas tank in his company van in the morning and then set the trip mileage meter. At the end of the day after all deliveries are made, he will fill the gas tank again and take note of both the mileage on the trip meter and the number of gallons of gas needed to fill the tank. The number of miles driven divided by the number of gallons used will give Annie her MPG information for this van. What is the van's MPG rating if it went 284 miles on 16 gallons of gas? _____

Annie has decided to replace all the old company vans with a newer model rated at 21 MPG. The delivery drivers like the new vans better, viewing the change as a positive development. The old vans will be sold off gradually, beginning with the highest-mileage vehicles. Annie thinks that the new vans will save the company 1,600 gallons of gasoline per year once all the old vans have been disposed of. If the company buys its fuel for $1.55 per gallon, how much money will be saved by not needing those 1,600 gallons of fuel each year? _____

More About Annie's MPG Study

Annie has had time to study the fleet of cars used by the sales force. The cars are all four-door luxury sedans, each equipped with air-conditioning and automatic transmission. Annie is concerned about these cars because all of them are "gas hogs." She thinks that operating this fleet has become wasteful when weighed against the company's overall finances. Annie would like to see them replaced with more fuel-efficient models. The sales force sedans average only 14 miles per gallon. Salespeople buy their gasoline at different locations all over the state, but the average cost is $1.59 per gallon. How much does it cost the company in fuel charges for a salesperson to drive one of these cars 84 miles? _____

HAPPY TO HELP!

Annie noticed that her own car was getting 21.5 miles per gallon before she had the regular suggested maintenance performed on the car. Her mechanic did all the normal maintenance work but also suggested that Annie try a new type of synthetic motor oil designed to improve fuel economy. After the car was serviced and the new oil added, Annie noticed that her car was now getting 23.25 miles per gallon. It did not seem like much of an increase, but then Annie realized that this was fuel economy she had previously been losing. How many more miles is Annie now able to travel on the same gallon of fuel? _____

Curious Student Discovers Old Measurement Units

Trevor came across the word *gill* while reading an excerpt from a historical journal. Trevor was already familiar with the word *gills* used for describing a fish's breathing apparatus. But in the context of the sentence, a *gill* appeared to relate to measurement. Trevor consulted an almanac to see if he could find a meaning for the word in the context of a measurement unit.

Trevor soon found that four gills combined to make one pint. It was apparent to Trevor that two gills would have to equal one cup. Trevor figured that at some point in time a gill must have satisfied the need for measuring small amounts of liquid without resorting to more precise ounce measures. How many gills would be needed to equal one gallon? _____

Trevor enjoys browsing through almanacs, especially when he is fortunate enough to discover new math-related words. (Trevor's friends think he needs more hobbies.) While looking through the almanac to find out about gills, Trevor discovered another measurement-related word, which had fallen out of common usage somewhat. He discovered that a *peck* is used for measuring dry goods. One peck is equal to eight quarts. If 32 quarts equal one bushel, then how many pecks does it take to equal one bushel? _____

More About Trevor and His Study of Measurements

Trevor's father thought Trevor was spending too much time indoors. Studying almanacs did not seem to him like a healthy pursuit for a normal school kid. That is why he asked Trevor to help him stack the wood order which had just been delivered to their house. By arrangement, a driver brings their firewood in a large truck and dumps it on the ground. It then has to be stacked in a place convenient to the house.

Trevor did not mind helping his father stack the wood. It gave him the opportunity to test what he knew about *cord* measurement for determining a quantity of firewood. Trevor knew that one cord of cut firewood, tightly stacked, should equal exactly 128 cubic feet. When they finished stacking the wood, much to his father's amazement, Trevor declared that they had been shorted on their wood order. His father had paid for three full cords of firewood. Trevor measured their new stack of firewood and found it to be 8 feet wide by 8 feet long by 4 feet tall. How many feet taller should the stack of wood have been in order to be the correct amount they had ordered?

_____

Trevor's father decided that having the boy along might be a good idea when he goes to buy lumber for an upcoming fine wood project. The specialty lumber store prices its wood by the board foot, a standard unit of measure describing a board that is one inch thick and measures 1 foot by 1 foot.

Trevor carefully measured all the pieces of wood selected by his father at the specialty lumber store. He arrived at a figure of 21.75 board feet. If this particular wood is priced at $12 per board foot, and sales tax is 8%, how much should Trevor's father owe for the lumber? _____

Difficult Time for Shampoo Inventors

Henry had the idea to produce shampoo in his garage and then market it locally. He brought in his friend Josh to help with the business. Henry bought a number of cleaning products to use in developing the shampoo. He and Josh eventually settled on using Lemony Dish Liquid as the base ingredient for the shampoo. Lemony Dish Liquid could be purchased at the wholesale club in 5-gallon containers, making it quite economical. The two settled on a perfume, Trace of Paris, as the fragrance for the shampoo. Trace of Paris is also available at their wholesale club in convenient quart containers. Another secret ingredient went into the shampoo formula, ground basil, which Henry got from his wife's backyard herb garden.

The shampoo was not well received by the places where Henry and Josh tried to sell it. Even people at the flea market did not want it. One person thought it might have good potential as a bug repellent. Henry spent $75.99 for a gross of 12-ounce plastic containers, $48.44 to have labels printed, $19.35 on cleaning products used for initial testing, $18.50 for Lemony Dish Liquid, $11.90 for Trace of Paris perfume, $17.50 for flea market booth rental, and $6 on new basil plants to replace the ones taken from his wife's herb garden. The money to purchase these supplies was taken from Henry's savings account. If the account originally had a balance of $356.16, how much is left in the account after the supplies were purchased? _____

Josh has been talking with the foreman at his place of work, Built-Fast Construction Company. Josh wants to help Henry with the lost shampoo investment, especially since Henry's wife did not react well when she found out about the shampoo venture. Josh thinks that his foreman might buy the 12 dozen bottles of shampoo to use as lubricant for drill bits on their job sites.

After talking with Josh, the foreman agreed to buy the "shampoo" for $1.19 per bottle. He wants the shampoo delivered in equal quantities to eight different job sites with a separate invoice prepared for each job site. How much will the invoice be for each job site?

_____

Dog Shopper Weighs Differences

Maude is thinking of buying a new dog.
Her old dog, Buffy, recently ran away after a 12-year
relationship. Maude is still perplexed as to what she did wrong but vows
to do better in meeting the needs of the new dog and making it happy as well. She
wants a dog that is small and will be able to accompany her when she goes to the
boutique, bank, and other places she frequents.

One important factor Maude must evaluate is the dog's size. Since she will carry this
new dog with her wherever she goes, it must be lightweight. That is one of the
reasons she favors Chihuahuas and Norfolk Terriers. Maude has read that most
Chihuahuas average 5 pounds, 12 ounces in weight, while Norfolk Terriers average 11
pounds, 4 ounces. A third dog, the Pomeranian, has also been under consideration at
an average weight of 6 pounds, 6 ounces. On average, how much additional weight
will Maude be carrying around if she chooses a Norfolk Terrier over a Chihuahua?

_____

A friend of Maude's, Estelle, has offered to give Maude a Great Dane. Estelle lost
patience with the dog after experiencing a series of accidents and behavior incidents.
The Great Dane, called Bantam, collapsed an armchair by jumping into it and also ate
a 9-pound dinner ham that was cooling on the
kitchen table. These incidents represent only a
few in a long string of misunderstandings.

Maude has decided to put aside her preference
for small dogs and give this one a try. Since the
dog is free, it sounds like a good deal to Maude!
Bantam weighs 165 pounds, so he will not be
able to sit on Maude's lap or travel in the car
with her when she shops. But Maude thinks
Bantam will make a much more serious guard
dog for her property. The vet has recommended
that Bantam eat 4 pounds, 8 ounces of dry dog
food per day. How many pounds of dry dog
food will Maude need on hand to feed Bantam for
two weeks? _____

"Horse Moving Is Our Business"

Interstate Horse Transport Company owns a fleet of specialized trucks used for moving horses. Their slogan is "Horse Moving Is Our Business." Interstate Horse will also transport expensive cattle, but its main business is in horses.

Interstate Horse charges $1,250 to move a horse cross-country. If the owner has more than one horse that needs to be transported to the same location, then each additional horse is billed out at a discounted price of $850. What would the total billed amount be for a horse owner sending five horses cross-country to the same location? _____

An accountant working for Interstate Horse Transport Company has been studying the company's books. While the company is very profitable, the accountant thinks that more work is needed to determine the true cost basis for each trip. The accountant has considered all expenses involved in paying salaries and operating the trucks. It costs Interstate Horse $.80 per mile on average to transport a horse.

The accountant thinks that the company should move to a system of quoting customers flat fees for mileage involved instead of per horse or varying fees depending on the destination involved. The accountant thinks that $1.25 per mile would represent a reasonable and profitable amount to charge customers. How much profit per mile would the accountant's suggestion mean for the company if the idea ends up being used?

_____

More About Interstate Horse Transport Company

Interstate Horse Transport Company has just agreed to deliver four rodeo bulls to a rodeo only several hundred miles away. They usually do not carry these kinds of animals but agreed to take on the job after the company that usually handles shipping these animals had an unexpected breakdown.

The bulls were loaded into one of Interstate Horse's livestock trailers, and the rodeo promoter paid $615 in advance to have the bulls moved. Unfortunately, the energetic bulls damaged the inside of the trailer en route to the rodeo. Interstate Horse will now have to pay $279.19 to repair the stalls and have a welder fix damage done to the trailer's metal work. The driver's pay for this job was $185, and gasoline to operate the truck on this trip cost Interstate Horse another $98.50. How much money did Interstate Horse Transport Company actually make for this transport job after the damage and expenses are considered? _____

Interstate Horse Transport Company just sold one of its old trucks to a private buyer. The truck brought $18,000, and the new owner appeared quite satisfied at this price. Interstate Horse will apply this money to the purchase of a new truck. The truck they have been considering has two extra horse stalls, which will make it a more profitable truck to put on the highway. The new truck is priced at $71,459. After they apply the $18,000 from their old truck to the new purchase, how much money will Interstate Horse still need to put toward the new truck purchase? _____

Grocery Manager Does the Math

Pete is the manager of Food and Drug Central. His store is one of many in a large midwestern grocery and drug store corporation. Pete is of the opinion that understanding math helps his store run smoothly. He tries to approach store situations in a logical way, always considering the math involved. How much time should it take an employee to perform a certain task? How should this product be priced to ensure a reasonable profit? How many displays can be arranged in a given space? These are just a few examples of the kinds of questions Pete deals with all day in his work.

Pete is looking at an empty space in front of one of the aisles. This spot is normally used for displaying a current store special. This time, Pete will use the space to showcase a newly introduced premium coffee brand. The floor space available measures 3 feet by 4 feet. Pete has instructed the stock clerk to stack the coffee cans no more than 5 feet high. Pete thinks that displays taller than that should be limited to paper towels and soft goods that do not pose a risk if they fall. How many cubic feet of space are available for this coffee display? _____

Pete has been experimenting with the price of lamb chops. He thinks that he has found a pricing strategy that works for this product. The cost on this product is $2.65 per pound when it arrives at Food and Drug Central. Pete has instructed the meat manager to price average-quality lamb chops at $6.99 per pound. If the lamb chops look like really premium cuts, Pete wants them priced at $8.69 per pound. How much more money per pound does the store make in profit on the premium cuts over the average cuts? _____

More About Pete the Grocery Manager

Pete has been studying the cost of labor at Food and Drug Central. The cost of labor includes anything paid to employees in salary or benefits. Pete thinks that several employees have been wasting sick days. He is especially irritated with Duncan, who has missed 12 days (all Mondays) clustered over a period of just a few months.

Employees at the store told Pete that Duncan sits on his couch watching football games all weekend and drinks heavily while doing it. That is why Duncan calls in sick so often on Mondays during the football season. Pete has figured that it costs the company a total of $96.50 per sick day in lost wages and productivity each time an employee is out sick. Pete was appalled when he figured what Duncan's absences had already cost the store. Pete does not mind when a person is really sick, but Duncan is completely abusing the sick-leave policy. How much have Duncan's absences cost the store?_____

Pete has decided to stop carrying all tobacco products in the store. He considers these products to pose dangerous health risks and does not want his store to be involved in their trade. Pete knows that some executives at the Food and Drug Central corporate office will question his decision. On average the store makes $885 per week in profits on the sale of tobacco products. Pete wants to stock new products that will make up for this loss of profit. How much money per year will Pete need to make from these new products to completely offset the lost tobacco profits? _____

Fishing Tournament Makes Big Splash

Burt has entered the First Annual Regional Sportsman's Fishing Tournament. The tournament is being sponsored by a group of area bait and tackle dealers. Prizes will be awarded for first, second, and third place finishes in each fish class. First-place prize in each fish class is $250! The entry fee is $45 for the tournament. Burt figures that he is the best fisherman in the area when it comes to catching catfish, so he views the entry fee as just something of a formality involved in collecting the prize money.

Burt's wife, Delores, does not share his opinion. She thinks that they have seen the last of the $45 entry fee. That is why Burt did not tell her that he spent another $8.49 on bait, $12.20 on a new spool of 30-pound line for landing the "big one," $26.55 to fill the boat's gas tank, and $14.78 to stock his ice chest with drinks for the tournament. How much money has Burt spent on this tournament so far? _____

On tournament day, Burt noticed that only first place in each fish division paid a cash prize. Second- and third-place prizes were items donated by the various fishing tackle stores involved in the tournament.

Burt was able to land a large catfish in his boat before the tournament's 5 p.m. finishing time. It was not the biggest catfish he had ever caught, but Burt figured that it might be enough to win the tournament. When Burt produced his fish for official weigh-in, he noticed another catfish was already on the leader board at 23 pounds, 3 ounces. Burt's fish weighed in at 22 pounds, 8 ounces on the official tournament scale. As second-place finisher, Burt won a year's subscription to a fishing magazine and a six-month supply of worms. How much weight had Burt's entry been beaten by? _____

Computer User Studies Printer Costs

Lisa's old printer recently stopped working. She decided that she would be better off to just buy a new printer. The warranty had expired on her old printer and she had no idea how expensive it might be to fix it. It would also have cost Lisa about $30 to have the printer packaged and sent to an authorized repair facility. Since she does a lot of work on her computer, shopping for a replacement printer became a priority.

Lisa looked at a lot of new printers but narrowed her choice to two printers. She likes the fact that they are both very fast. One printer costs $209 and is rated to print 8 pages per minute. The other printer is slightly cheaper at $199, but it prints only 5 pages per minute. Lisa is trying to decide if the faster printer is worth the extra money. She has thought of an example printing job to use in comparing the printers. If Lisa wants to print a document that is 40 pages in length, how much longer will the slower printer take to do the job? _____

Lisa decided to go with the cheaper printer, even though she knew it would be slower in getting the print jobs done. What she had not realized at the time was the

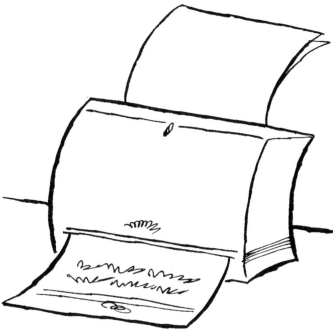

difference in cost for the cartridges that go with each printer. A cartridge for the printer she bought costs $38.95. But a cartridge for the more expensive printer she had previously considered, but decided against, is only $19.95. Both cartridges are rated at printing the same number of pages, 500. Lisa suddenly realized that each time she has to replace an empty printer cartridge, it will cost her more money than if she had gone with the more expensive printer! How much more money will it cost Lisa in added cartridge expense each time she has to replace a cartridge for the less expensive printer?

_____

Advertising Firm Scrambles to Keep Up

Plimpton and Drake are partners in an advertising firm. They charge clients $300 per hour for advertising consultations. These consultations consist mostly of the two of them sitting with a client and tossing around silly ideas until the client reacts positively to something. Most of Drake's ideas are stolen from competitors. Plimpton is fond of reworking material from the 1950s and 1960s that his father developed as the original owner of the firm.

Plimpton and Drake have just finished a meeting with a client. The meeting lasted 80 minutes but went very badly near the end. The client stormed out, saying that he was not going to pay $300 an hour for this kind of lousy advice. If this client refuses to pay his bill, how much money will the firm lose on this consultation? _____

Drake is certain that a vacation would help both of them to relax and to recharge their creative batteries. He also likes the idea of traveling to a foreign country and scooping up advertising ideas that people in the United States will not have already seen.

Plimpton is not sure that they can afford to take the time off. He points out that in the last year the firm's client base has dropped from 214 paying clients to its present low of only 59 paying clients. On average, each paying client is worth $2,355 per year to the firm. The two decided they must get serious about their work as soon as the vacation is finished. How much income have they lost in the last year due to the loss of so many clients? _____

More About Drake and Plimpton

Drake and Plimpton returned from their vacation feeling refreshed and ready to begin work anew. While they were gone their firm's receptionist quit and also left a note saying that 12 more customers had resigned from the firm. This did not worry Drake, as he had stolen enough advertising ideas on vacation to last them at least several months. Plimpton immediately called the employment agency and asked them to send over some new candidates to interview for the receptionist job.

The agency representative called back a little while later to tell Plimpton that they could send over only 5 candidates for interview. Word had gotten around the employment agency about work conditions at their advertising firm. Not many people wanted to work there, since it was rumored that the firm would be out of business soon. If it takes Plimpton 20 minutes to interview each potential receptionist, how long should he set aside for the interviews, allowing a 10-minute break between each one? _____

LET'S EAT!

Drake and Plimpton did begin to get alarmed when their accountant called late one afternoon to say that he was dropping them as customers since the advertising firm was now broke. Drake suggested that they use whatever money was left in the petty cash fund to have a pizza delivered so that they could work late. Plimpton thought that this was an excellent idea, since it would give them a chance to eat while they developed a new business plan. The petty cash fund contains $22.54. How much will be left in it after the pizza delivery driver is paid $14.79 for the pizza plus a $2.50 tip?

_____

Handmade Clog Shop Does Okay

Janice and Patty own the Handmade Clogs by Janice & Patty shop. The two make clogs and sandals for customers who like wearing handmade shoes. Janice and Patty have found a brisk market for their product since their small store first opened.

Their first year, often the hardest for a new business, has been pretty good so far. The good results have given Janice a sense of relief, especially since she signed a one-year lease on the store when they first began the clog shop. The shop's lease for one year cost $6,300, with equal rent payments to be made by the third day of each month. How much is the monthly rent at Handmade Clogs by Janice & Patty? _____

Both partners can make a fine pair of clogs, but Janice is a bit faster in her work than Patty. Janice can make a pair of clogs from start to finish in 45 minutes. It usually takes Patty 60 minutes to produce a comparable pair. This time difference is not a point of contention between the two. Janice and Patty both realize that each of them works at a different pace. Patty is often faster than Janice with other store tasks, but each has something important to contribute to the shop. In the time it takes Janice to make 8 pairs of clogs, how many will Patty have been able to produce? _____

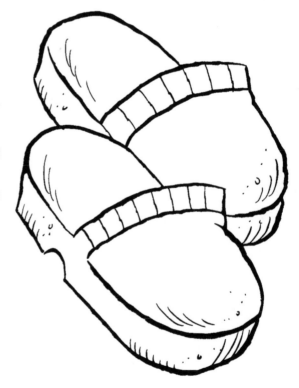

More About Handmade Clogs by Janice & Patty

Leather and wood represent the two main components for clogs made in the shop. The partners felt strongly about sticking with natural materials whenever possible in crafting their product. They have gradually fallen into a routine around the shop, with a particular task falling to whoever seems best at dealing with it. For example, Patty is the one who screens and purchases all the raw materials from their suppliers.

Patty selects only the strongest hides when buying leather for the shop. She also prefers larger hides, since those allow more options in how they may be cut and put to use. The hides come to the shop in an irregular shape. Patty looks at each one and tries to determine its usable area. She knows the irregularly shaped edges will largely be cut away, leaving what is essentially a rectangular piece of leather for production. Patty has just purchased a hide that measures 2,021 square inches in total surface area. The hide has a usable rectangular-shaped area of 38 inches by 46 inches. How many square inches of unusable material are there on this particular leather hide?

_____

WORK WORK WORK!

Janice and Patty put in long hours at the shop. Handmade Clogs by Janice & Patty opens for business at 9 a.m. and closes at 6 p.m. Monday through Friday. On Saturdays they keep shorter hours. The shop is open from 10 a.m. until 4 p.m. One of the two partners must be at the shop whenever it is open. Ordinarily, the two are both in the shop, working hard to produce clogs and sandals. Their schedule does not leave a lot of flexibility for taking time off. How many hours per week is the shop open for business?

_____

New Jobs Mean Change in Work Habits?

Drake and Plimpton were forced to close their advertising agency. None of the business ventures they tried together afterwards worked, although Drake's idea of selling fine jewelry door to door nearly succeeded. They had to give that up when Drake left a briefcase with expensive samples in the back of a cab by mistake. Things were looking very bleak until Plimpton saw an ad for vacation time-share salespeople.

The sales manager at Vacation Getaways Unlimited thought Drake and Plimpton had all the necessary qualifications for succeeding in time-share sales. Plimpton agreed, especially since most of their previous work experience also involved selling things nobody seemed to want. The time-share jobs pay a straight 5% commission on units sold. The time-share manager said that a good salesperson should have no trouble selling $1,000,000 worth of time-shares per year. How much money can Drake and Plimpton each expect to make selling time-shares if the sales manager's estimate is correct? _____

As with many other things, the time-share sales did not work out for Drake and Plimpton. The sales manager fired them both after the two accidentally set a model unit on fire trying to cook during their lunch break. Plimpton put out the grease fire very quickly with a fire extinguisher, but smoke damage had already ruined $8,500 worth of furniture and draperies.

The sales manager has threatened to hold back half of their last paychecks to pay the insurance deductible for the fire damage. Drake was due $1,225 in commission on the sale of a 3-bedroom unit. Plimpton was supposed to receive $950 for selling a studio unit with an ocean view. If the sales manager does as he has threatened, how much money will Plimpton lose from his last paycheck? _____

Salesperson Wanted

Jackie works full-time selling furniture at The Lazy Couch Furniture Outlet. She is paid a salary of $200 per week. Jackie also receives a bonus commission on every furniture sale she makes. This commission is computed as a small percentage of the selling price of whatever furniture items Jackie has sold that week. The owner of Lazy Couch Furniture Outlet thinks the salespeople work harder to close deals since they have the added commission to look forward to as part of their pay.

The amount of money Jackie makes in commissions varies from week to week, depending on how much furniture she is able to sell. Her commission rate is 3% of total furniture sales. Several salespeople who have been with the company longer are paid a 4% commission rate, but Jackie has not been with the company long enough to be eligible for this higher commission rate. What will Jackie's total pay be during a week when she sells $3,200 in furniture items? _____

Jackie is not sure she wants to stay with the furniture business. She interviewed with Clean Chem, a company that manufactures industrial chemicals. Clean Chem has several openings for salespeople, but Jackie is concerned by their compensation plan. Clean Chem's sales manager explained to Jackie that the sales position has no fixed salary, so her pay would be based entirely on sales commissions. This made Jackie a bit nervous, since she is used to having a guaranteed salary, but she is still seriously considering Clean Chem's offer.

Clean Chem pays salespeople a 6% commission on all chemical sales. The sales manager at Clean Chem told Jackie that she could expect to sell $300,000 worth of chemicals during her first year with the company. That amount could be expected to grow as Jackie's customer base grows. How much money would Jackie earn in commissions in her first year at Clean Chem if the sales manager's prediction is correct? _____

Investigator Knows History

All of Manning's friends and acquaintances think that he has the most interesting kind of job. Manning always tells them that he will let them go down into the crawl space underneath a house the next time it needs to be done. In his work, Manning conducts historical investigations of properties. His firm, New England Residential Antiquities Research, is frequently called upon to investigate the history associated with old houses. By using old maps, titles, architectural clues, and other resources, Manning is often able to trace the history of a property and its buildings back as far the 1600s.

Manning charges $60 per hour for what he terms "background research." This covers any kind of reading, museum research, or other scholarly investigation he performs. Manning charges $80 per hour for "on-site research." This includes walking a property to look for clues, conducting a research dig at a site, or examining any physical aspects of a house. How much would the total bill be for a client who had 3.50 hours of background research and 1.25 hours of on-site research performed in regard to some property? _____

Manning recently conducted research on an old stone foundation, which the owners of the property had heard was once a tavern. Through documents, Manning was able to confirm that a tavern had, indeed, once stood on the site. He discovered that it was built in 1729.

Tax records indicated that the property was passed down to subsequent generations of the same family. Additional records showed the tavern had extensive additions made in 1836, with the total square footage being nearly doubled. In 1855 ownership of the property passed from the original family to a new owner. Manning could find no other documents regarding the tavern until a fire report in 1891 listed it as being totally destroyed by fire that same year. Manning told the property owners he would keep his eyes open for any further information that might turn up. How many years separate the time when the additions were made from the fire report? _____

More About Manning and His Research

Manning has been asked to research a piece of waterfront property in an old New England village. The small brick house was thought to be a restored office for an old maritime business. Manning was told by the property owner that rumors had long circulated of a once-thriving maritime business from about 1790 on the site, with a large pier and possible boatyard there at one time as well. Rumors of smuggling and pirates were also associated with the property. In general, Manning is suspicious of rumors passed on to him by property owners. Manning insists on building a property's historical profile strictly based on his own research.

Manning was able to trace the true history of the property in a short time. The first document he found for the property was a sales transaction. In 1705 the property was deeded to a fish merchant. For many years it was a site where fish were sold in an open-air market. A farmer bought the property from the fish merchant in 1749 and turned it into a horse paddock. In 1813 the property was sold to a businessman who immediately had warehouses built for storing marine shipments. The warehouse business ended abruptly with a fire in 1841. The present brick house was actually built in 1890, a modest little home once belonging to the village schoolmaster. How many years was the property used as either a warehouse or a fish market?

Manning has been doing historical research on properties and houses for 33 years. His partner, Mr. Simms, is still working at age 72, with 41 years in the business. It was Mr. Simms who first founded New England Residential Antiquities Research. Their junior partner, William, has only 9 years in the field but is learning rapidly. How many years of combined experience can New England Residential Antiquities Research boast having among the three partners? _____

Fence Company Takes Pride in Fast Work

Larry works for Fast Fences, a company that specializes in the installation of chain link fences.

Fast Fences has built a reputation around giving the customer a precise date on which the work will be completed. With the proper preparation, Fast Fences can have most house yards and smaller commercial properties completely finished in a single day.

Part of Larry's job involves traveling to the customer's location, measuring the property, and providing an on-the-spot price quote. His price quote must include a promised completion date if the customer elects to have the work performed. Larry has promised a one-day installation to a property owner with a rectangular yard measuring 120 feet by 148 feet. How many feet of fence will Larry's crew have to install in one workday to complete this job? _____

For another project, Larry quoted a total price of $2,127 to enclose a customer's entire yard. The quote also included two pedestrian gates, one remote-controlled automobile gate, and Fast Fences' speedy one-day installation.

This customer was not convinced that Fast Fences should do the work. He pointed out that another fence company had quoted only $4.29 per foot for the completed job. Larry took another look at his figures. The fence would follow the perimeter of this customer's yard, a total distance of 424 feet. How much will Larry have to reduce his price quote for the job if he intends to match the other fence company's price quote? _____

More About Larry's Work at Fast Fences

Larry was called out to look at doing a fence job for a customer with an L-shaped corner lot.

Larry arrived at the site to find a very large, six-sided yard, just as had been described to him on the telephone. Larry measured the yard's longest sides at 500 and 600 feet respectively. The owner of the property assured Larry that his yard was laid out at right angles. Larry was able to verify this when he found two of the property's other sides to be 300 feet (each) in length and the two remaining sides to be 250 feet (each) in length.

Before making any calculations, Larry could already tell that the work needed for this yard could not be completed in a single day. His crew can only handle installing a maximum of 600 feet of fence per day. If this customer decides to use Fast Fences for this job, how many days does Larry need to tell the customer it will take to complete the job? _____

Larry has been exhausted from all the work orders coming in to Fast Fences lately. He has been pestering the owner of Fast Fences to hire another worker for his crew, so the work load can be spread out a bit.

The owner of Fast Fences has had to pay a total of 40 hours in overtime pay to Larry's crew in the last week alone. Workers in Larry's crew ordinarily make $8.50 per hour. If overtime pay is 1.5 times the regular rate, how much cheaper would it have been for the owner to have been paying another full-time worker instead of paying all this overtime? _____

Miles Give Way to Kilometers

Norman is familiar with the metric system. He has often used it in school and knows that it is just another way of measuring various quantities. On a recent trip to Canada with his family, Norman was not surprised to see distances shown in kilometers on road signs. He noticed that the city they were traveling to first was listed as being 240 kilometers away.

Norman always keeps a journal on these trips. It is a good way for him to later remember the places he went and any noteworthy events. Norman remembered that one mile is equal to approximately 1.6 kilometers. He thought that it would be convenient to convert any kilometer figures encountered to miles for his journal entries, since he is more familiar with miles. How many miles will Norman mark in his travel log for this leg of the trip? _____

Norman noticed that his car's speedometer had an interior row of numbers arranged below the more prominent miles-per-hour notations. He assumed that these numbers represented kilometers per hour. Norman decided to spot check one of the pairs of numbers to see if his assumption was correct. What miles-per-hour figure should correspond to the 40-kilometers-per-hour mark on the car's speedometer? _____

HIT THE ROAD!

Computer Buyer Evaluates Options

Patrick is buying a desktop computer.
The company he is ordering from builds the computer
only after it is ordered by the customer. This allows the customer to
determine how the computer will be equipped. Patrick can decide how much
memory his computer will have, what kind of processor will be installed, the size
monitor his system will have, etc.

The basic computer system Patrick chose costs $899. He added a memory upgrade to
the package at a cost of $89 and a slightly faster processor for an additional $129.
Patrick also upgraded the speakers for $69 and increased the size of the monitor from
15 inches to 19 inches at a cost of $179. Patrick even went with overnight shipping at
a cost of $79, since he was anxious to have the computer as soon as it was ready.
How much money in all is Patrick paying to get his new computer system? _____

After his computer was delivered, Patrick noticed a brochure that had been included in the box. The brochure explained an additional warranty available from the company. His computer system already came with a basic warranty. The additional warranty offered in the brochure appeared to cover much more. For a one-time payment of $144, Patrick would receive guaranteed next-day, in-home service for his computer during the first two years. A temporary replacement computer was offered under the warranty if the technician was unable to fix the computer on-site. This sounded like a good deal to Patrick, but he was curious as to how much money on average the extra warranty worked out to be for each month of the warranty plan. What is the average cost per month for the additional warranty? _____

Space in Short Supply

Elizabeth, Susan, and Kelly are roommates. They share a large town house, due to expensive rents in the city. Each roommate pays an equal share of the rent, and decisions about the town house are made by majority vote. Recently, space has become something of a problem. Everybody has been accumulating furniture and knick-knacks and open space is in very short supply.

The group decided that each roommate should reduce the number of books kept in the town house. Unwanted books will be donated to an upcoming library book drive. Elizabeth was put in charge of packing the books to take to the library. While collecting everybody's books and packing them in boxes, Elizabeth noticed that the donated books exactly fit a 2 : 3 : 4 ratio. A total of 27 books was donated by the roommates. How many books did the person who contributed the most books put into the donation? _____

Susan is in charge of finances for the town house. Each roommate equally shares the cost of all rent and utilities. It is Susan's job to keep track of what bills are due and also to write checks to cover those expenses. Susan recently received a notice from the landlord. The rent on the town house is being raised from $760 per month to $880 per month. Susan must now figure how this affects each roommate's share. How much more money will each roommate now need to contribute each month to cover the new increase in rent? _____

More About the Roommates

Elizabeth, Susan, and Kelly have arranged with the landlord to have the basement remodeled. Previously, the basement was used only for storage and as a laundry room. A bathroom, new lighting fixtures, and carpeting are among the things being added. The landlord has agreed to pay for these things since it was promised when Susan first signed the lease. Susan thinks that the basement room could be rented to a fourth roommate once all the work is finished.

Each roommate is now paying $420 per month for her share of the combined rent and utility bills. If a new roommate moves into the basement and accepts responsibility for one-fourth of the total rent and utility bills, how much money will each roommate then be paying for her share of the monthly expenses? _____

HEY-YOU DO THE MATH!

Neither Elizabeth, Susan, nor Kelly was able to locate a compatible roommate for the available space. Only a few people they knew seemed like good prospects, and none of those wanted to live in a basement. The three have decided to make the basement into a recreation room. The basement has dimensions of 14 feet by 20 feet. Not all of that space is usable for recreation, though. The washer, dryer, and clothes-folding table take up 30 square feet of floor space. How much floor space is available for the roommates' recreation plans? _____

"Busy" Characterizes Restaurant Work

Janice works as a waitress at the Deep Fried Chicken Shack. It is one in a chain of restaurants that specializes in fried chicken. In fact, fried chicken is the only main course served at Deep Fried Chicken Shack, but the restaurant does offer over 20 different side dishes. When she first began working at the restaurant, it took Janice quite some time to remember the order codes for all these dishes when filling out order slips for the cooks.

Janice is generally responsible for eight tables during a shift. Six of those tables will seat only four people each. Janice's other tables will seat up to eight people each, making for a real headache on busier days. What is the maximum number of patrons that could be seated in Janice's section when things are really busy? _____

Whenever Janice has a party of six or more at one table in her section, the restaurant imposes a mandatory 15% gratuity (tip) and requires the group's bill to be on a single tab. Patrons are made aware of this policy when they are seated. It prevents Janice from running herself ragged for an hour trying to please a large group, only to be short-changed with a cheap tip. Janice has just waited on a group of eight people whose total bill came to $142.40. What is the minimum tip Janice can expect to receive from this party?

_____

YOU WANT FRIES WITH THAT?

More About Janice's Work at the Restaurant

Deep Fried Chicken Shack considers tips to be a part of the overall compensation package for waiters and waitresses. Janice is also paid $100 per week by the restaurant, since the management knows that they would have trouble getting an experienced waitress to work solely for tips. In addition to her salary, Janice also receives medical insurance from the restaurant, an added benefit not enjoyed by all workers.

Janice made a total of $12,060 from her job at Deep Fried Chicken Shack last year. Tips turned out to make up more of her overall pay than the money paid to her by the restaurant. How much money did Janice receive in tips last year? _____

A party of four spend the better part of an afternoon at a table in Janice's section. The group ordered only desserts and coffee. They spent most of the afternoon talking and motioning at her for free coffee refills. Janice was quite exasperated at the table being tied up for so long and having to cater to them for such a long time. When the group finally left the restaurant, Janice was given a $9 tip! The group's total bill had amounted to only $15. The usual tip expected by a waitress is only 15% of the bill. What percentage of this group's bill did this tip represent?

_____

School Elections: Serious Business?

Trixie attends Academy High School. For the most part, Trixie could care less about school politics or positions in student government. But her opinion in this matter recently changed after talking to a family friend. It seems that this friend's nephew was, by all accounts, a dull person with an uneventful high school record. But he was admitted to a prestigious university because of his prominent position in school government. Since Trixie wants to attend a high-profile college, this has given her cause to think about the upcoming student government elections at her school.

In Trixie's school, 107 students are juniors. Juniors have a proportionate number of seats allotted on the student council. The council has 15 seats, and Trixie thinks that she would have a good chance of being elected as one of the junior class representatives. How many seats are set aside for juniors if the total student body numbers 535? _____

Robert, one of Trixie's close friends, has been telling people that once Trixie is elected, they will have a real voice in student government. For a modest campaign donation of only $15, Robert assured students that Trixie would always be responsive to their needs and concerns. Robert managed to collect $285 from students interested in having special influence before Trixie found out what he was doing and put a stop to the practice. She insisted that Robert return all the money he had collected. How many students are due refunds? _____

Truck Buyer Gets Less Than Bargained For

Andy recently purchased a new pickup truck. He had a number of requirements when choosing his new vehicle, including four-wheel drive, extended cab, and automatic transmission. Andy also selected a truck with a large eight-cylinder engine. At the time Andy did not realize that these were all features that generally contribute to reduced fuel economy. Andy has been driving his truck for several weeks and was quite disappointed to find out that the truck was getting only 18 miles per gallon.

Andy decided to test his truck's gas mileage again on a weekend fishing trip. He wants to determine how many miles per gallon the truck will get while towing his fishing boat. After the fishing trip was over, Andy checked his notes and found that the truck used 21 gallons of gas to travel 320.25 miles. How many miles per gallon did his truck get while towing the boat? _____

KEEP ON TRUCKIN'!

While Andy is satisfied with his truck, he also has tried doing several things over a period of time to improve the truck's fuel economy. Sometimes, simple things can increase a vehicle's MPG performance. Andy makes certain that the tires are always properly inflated, and he has stopped gunning the accelerator pedal when pulling out of driveways and parking lots. Andy also bought a vinyl snap cover for his truck bed to reduce air resistance. Andy thinks that these changes have been working to increase his fuel economy. Recently, he noted that the truck went 435.6 miles on 22 gallons of gas. How many miles per gallon (MPG) does that work out to be? _____

Farm's Variety Proves Successful

Sidney often helps her father around their farm. Their farm, Greenfield Pastures, is really not a full-scale dairy operation. Sidney's mother makes specialty cheeses as a sideline business. Their four dairy cows come to the barn very early every morning to be milked. Sidney frequently gets up to help her father with the milking, especially if other chores need doing as well.

It takes only a little while to milk the cows since it is done by machine. Sidney has noticed that the four cows usually produce a total of 10½ gallons of milk during these morning milking sessions. The milk produced is usually accumulated for several days in the barn's large refrigerator until Sidney's mother is ready to make a batch of cheese. On average, how many gallons of milk is each cow producing during the morning milking session? _____

Sidney's mother operates a small store on their property, the Greenfield Pastures Store. She keeps only morning hours at the store. Sidney's mother sells a variety of products in the store, all produced entirely at Greenfield Pastures. These include honey, cheese, ice cream, seasonal produce, and other farm-related products. One year Sidney and her mother made blackberry jam for the store from a 50-gallon batch of blackberries, which was taken in trade. Sidney's mother has developed a loyal clientele for her products.

The homemade cheese is in especially high demand and is usually the first item to sell out when the store opens. People have suggested that they should increase cheese production, but Sidney's mother thinks it would ruin the level of quality. Their cheese is priced at $5.50 per pound. It is sold in blocks that weigh 2½ pounds each. How much is a 2½-pound block of their cheese in the store? _____

More About Sidney and Greenfield Pastures

Sidney's father is considering the purchase of a 12-acre pasture. The pasture is located adjacent to Greenfield Pastures, which makes owning the land an ideal situation. The extra land could be used for additional grazing for their dairy cows or would make it possible to increase their flock of sheep. Sidney went with her father to inspect the property, and it looks like good, level land with quality grass and very few weeds.

The owner of this pastureland is asking $40,000 for the property. Sidney's father is planning to offer the owner $37,200. If the property's owner accepts the offer, how much per acre will Sidney's father be paying for the pastureland? _____

Sidney and her father have harvested the hay in one of the smaller hay fields at Greenfield Pastures. The hay was baled into bales weighing about 45 pounds each. The total yield for this field was 220 bales. Forty of those bales will be kept for feeding to their own livestock. They will sell the remaining bales for $4.80 each, since they expect to harvest more hay during the course of the summer. How much money will Sidney's father receive from the sale of this hay cutting?

_____

Cook Adjusts Recipes

Mason is making his favorite recipe for chicken marinade. He likes to prepare the marinade the day before he actually intends to broil the chicken, so that the chicken can soak in the marinade overnight. Mason has his marinade recipe committed to memory. He uses ¼ cup of Worcestershire sauce, ½ cup of red wine, ¼ cup of sugar, 2 tablespoons of pepper, and 4 tablespoons of olive oil. This recipe is enough for preparing one serving of chicken, ideal since Mason usually cooks for just himself.

Mason is having three friends over for dinner and wants to adjust his chicken marinade recipe to accommodate the increased number of people. Right now, Mason is checking the quantities he has on hand of each item that goes into the marinade recipe. How much red wine will Mason need once the recipe is adjusted to accommodate the increased number of people? _____

Mason also decided to prepare a special dessert for his small dinner party. The dessert he selected was a difficult-to-prepare chocolate dish with numerous ingredients. The complicated recipe was listed as yielding eight servings. One of the ingredients listed in the recipe was 1¾ pounds of semi-sweet chocolate. Mason plans to reduce this recipe to provide himself and his three guests with one serving each. How much semi-sweet chocolate will Mason need for the scaled-down recipe?

_____

COOKING IS AN ART!

More About Mason's Recipes

Mason got through his recent dinner party with compliments all around. Everybody thought the chicken turned out exceptionally well. One of Mason's guests even had a recipe she shared with him for a lamb marinade. Since Mason is always interested in fine marinades, he jotted down the ingredient list as she spoke: 1½ cups of olive oil, 2¼ cups of white wine, 4 tablespoons of thyme, 2 tablespoons of garlic, and 2 tablespoons of pepper. Mason immediately noticed that this recipe had no sugar or Worcestershire sauce, ingredients that give marinades a sweeter taste. He did not mention it to the dinner guest at the time, but Mason was already planning to change her recipe to suit his own taste.

Later that week Mason decided to try the lamb marinade recipe to see if it was any good. Right away, he noticed that the recipe he had been given was listed as being enough to prepare lamb sufficient for six people. He first had to convert all the quantities to the right amounts for preparing lamb for just one person. How much white wine does Mason need for the adjusted lamb marinade recipe? _____

A CULINARY MASTER-PIECE!

Mason finds himself worn out from all the fancy cooking and entertaining he has been doing lately. At the supermarket where he shops, he noticed a two-pound container of refrigerated cookie dough in the deli section. Mason normally cringes at these kinds of prepared-in-advance foods. But in his exhausted state, he has decided to give the cookie dough a try.

The entire container is listed as being enough to make 60 cookies. Mason wants to use just enough of the dough to make 24 cookies. How many ounces of dough should Mason separate out on his kitchen scales in order to make the number of cookies he wants? _____

This Agent Is No Spy

Hugh is a real-estate agent with Hilltop Realty Company. Hugh's specialty is selling real-estate properties held in the estates of deceased clients. He also handles a number of properties that are involved in bank foreclosures or legal litigation. Hugh enjoys the challenges involved in handling properties mired in complicated legal issues. He also likes spending long hours reading contracts, researching titles, and studying zoning laws. Hugh's colleagues at the realty company think that he is a really strange fellow, but Hugh has made something of a reputation for himself in the community as the agent to go to if you have a really difficult real-estate transaction pending.

Hugh has just sold a piece of foreclosed property for a bank. The property brought $212,000. Excited bank executives have begun calling Hugh their "secret agent" because he is so adept at quickly finding buyers for their difficult properties. Hugh received a 7% commission on this sale. How much money does that represent?

_____

Hugh was recently called in to look at a piece of residential property involved in an estate dispute. A reclusive 109-year-old man died, leaving all his great-grandchildren a share of the property. (The man had managed to outlive all of his children and grandchildren.) Hugh was called in because the heirs could agree on nothing, except that a fast sale of the property was needed.

To complicate matters, most people in the community thought that the gothic-looking house was haunted. The old house also needed a number of repairs, as it was in very poor condition. None of these factors was a problem for Hugh. He quickly sold the house to a fortune-teller who had just moved to town and pocketed a 5.5% commission on the $149,000 sale price. How much money did Hugh make from the sale of this house? _____

Auction Draws Interest

Alfred has a few unwanted items around the house that he would like to get rid of. He has been visiting online auction sites and thinks that he has found a site that is right for the items that he wants to sell.

Alfred is going to put an antique camera up for auction on this site. It costs the seller a flat fee of $2 to list an item of modest value such as Alfred's camera. If the item sells at auction, then the site collects a 12% commission on the sale price. If Alfred's antique camera fetches a high bid of $220 on this auction site, how much money will it have cost Alfred to sell this camera? _____

Alfred has listed several other items with this same auction site since he sold the antique camera. All his items are of modest value, but Alfred noticed that the site handles many very expensive items. He took a few moments to study the auction site's fee structure for expensive items.

The site charges the seller $50 to list any item with a minimum bid of $10,000 or more. The seller also pays a 7% commission on the sale price if the item sells. The buyer pays a 15% commission on the selling price of the item. Alfred thinks that the online auction site has a good deal going for it since money is collected from both the buyer and the seller. How much money does the online auction site collect from the sale of a $10,000 item? _____

51

Math Invades Art Class

Lindsey is an art teacher at the Russell Bates Academy of Fine Art. She normally teaches watercolor classes and the occasional portrait class. Lindsey also knows a little about pottery, and she has been asked to fill in for the regular pottery teacher who is out sick.

Instructions have been left for her to use a special batch of clay for today's class. Lindsey located the special clay, a large cube-shaped piece sitting on a wheeled cart in the pottery storage room. The cube is a rather good-sized chunk of clay, measuring 18 inches on a side. Lindsey sees that there are eight students on the class roster; this will make cutting the clay into equal pieces an easy task. She will just cut the cube in half, then cut each of those pieces into quarters. How many cubic inches of clay will each student be given to work with? _____

Lindsey frequently orders fine art paper in large rolls since it is more economical than buying regular pads of paper. The rolls also give her the option of cutting irregular-sized pieces of paper so that students can get experience working with paper of unusual sizes. Lindsey has just taken a roll of paper that is 36 inches wide and cut off a piece that is 50 inches long. She plans to cut this paper into three equal sheets with a short side of 12 inches. It will provide the three students in her advanced landscapes class the chance to work with a piece of paper that is narrow but also very long. How many square inches of space will be available on each of the sheets Lindsey will cut for the advanced landscapes class? _____

IT'S PUTTY IN MY HANDS!

More About Lindsey's Art Class

Lindsey is in the process of placing an art supplies order. She ordinarily orders from one of two companies. Both companies stock the same brands at similar prices. Figuring which place will be the cheapest on a particular order usually depends on which company is running a sale or which company is better on shipping charges.

The items Lindsey wants will cost $188.75 at Starving Artist Discount Art Supply. They pay all shipping charges if merchandise orders are over $200, but they charge $10 shipping for orders under $200. Lindsey's art supplies will cost only $180 at Crazy Bob's Art Discount Store, but they charge a flat rate of 8% of the total order for shipping. On this art supplies order, how much money will be saved by going with Crazy Bob's instead of Starving Artist Discount? _____

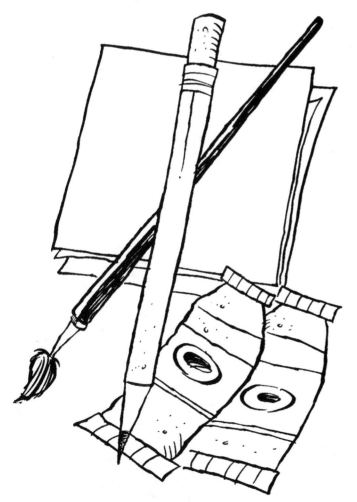

Lindsey ordered a new storage cabinet for her art room. It seems like there is seldom enough storage space for all the different art supplies. This is especially true since art materials are frequently ordered for a special project, then must be stored when all the supplies are not completely consumed during the project.

The new cabinet will have 30 cubic feet of interior storage space. It sounds like a lot, but Lindsey already has enough loose items to completely fill the thing! If the interior of the cabinet is 5 feet tall and 3 feet wide, how deep is it?

_____

Novice Investor Learns Expensive Lesson

Lenny has been watching the financial channels on television, trying to learn more about stocks. He has also seen a lot of commercials for online stock trading. Lenny thinks that a lot of people must be making fortunes from trading stocks. Friends have told Lenny that much of what he sees on television is hype, invented to separate people from their money. But Lenny has decided to try things out for himself.

Lenny took $10,000 from his savings account and opened an online stock trading account. He can make stock trades by paying just a $9.95 commission! Lenny knows that a share of stock is a small piece of ownership in a company, but he knows little beyond that. Anxious to get started, Lenny bought shares in a company the first day his trading account opened. He bought 80 shares of the company at a price of $40 per share. He also paid the $9.95 commission fee. What was Lenny's total cost for this stock purchase? _____

One of the first things Lenny noticed was that stock prices were listed on the exchanges as whole numbers, whole numbers with fractions, or just as fractions alone, depending on the current price of the stock. He learned that a quote of "35 and a ½" actually meant that the price of that stock was $35.50.

Many times, Lenny found himself trying to figure the difference in prices of various stocks in an effort to study their respective values. How much difference would Lenny find in the price of a stock quoted at 28⅝ and another quoted at 35⅛?

_____

More About Lenny and His Stock Trading

At first, Lenny did not pay much
attention to terms such as *earnings*, *dividends*, *market
caps*, and other financial jargon he heard bandied about on television.
He just took his original investment of $10,000 and used it to trade stocks based on
guesses he made about the companies or rumors he read about on message boards.
Lenny's first group of stock trades lost a total of $6,833.70 when the stocks were sold.

Later, Lenny came to realize that his method of selecting stocks was reckless and that
he was ignoring many factors important for determining the underlying value of a
stock. He was able to recoup $2,212.55 of his losses before liquidating all of his stocks.
How much of Lenny's original investment remains? _____

HEY...WHERE'D THE MONEY GO?

Lenny was eventually able to make one
good stock selection (or guess, depending
on how it is viewed). After a great deal of
study, Lenny bought 100 shares of an oil
company he had researched, paying 50¾
per share. Later he was able to sell this
stock at a price of $61¼ per share. This one
profitable transaction gave Lenny some
cause for hope! The usual commission fee
of $9.95 applied to both the purchase of
this stock and the sale of this stock. How
much profit did Lenny make on the oil
company stock? _____

Horse Terminology Conceals Underlying Math

One of Daphne's friends is a dedicated horse racing fan. Daphne has been to the track a number of times with Millard. Millard takes the races quite seriously, trying to predict the outcome of each race in advance. After a race he tries to analyze the performance of the horses involved. Daphne is far less serious about the horse races. She enjoys seeing the horses paraded before each race. Daphne also likes watching the horses run the races. She does not care anything about betting on the outcome of the races, but she would like to know what some of the horse terminology commonly used at the track actually means. It seems that each time she is at the track, the air is abuzz with words like *furlong, scratch, hands, long shot,* and other track parlance.

Daphne has just learned that the word *hand* is actually a measurement used for describing the height of a horse at the withers, a place above the horse's shoulders. Each hand represents four inches in height. What is the height in feet and inches of a horse described as 16½ hands? _____

Daphne heard the track announcer call the next race a "six-furlongs event." Millard was away at that moment making a wager, so Daphne saved her question until he returned. Millard explained to her that one furlong is a distance of 660 feet. It seemed amazing to Daphne that the horses were able to cover this distance so quickly. If a full mile is 5,280 feet, what portion of a mile do the horses cover in a 6-furlong event? _____

GIDDYUP!

Recycling Makes Sense . . . and Money!

Claudia accumulates aluminum cans and certain types of glass for recycling. In the area where she lives, there are a number of places she can turn in recyclable materials for cash. Claudia usually waits until she has a large load before redeeming the materials. It ordinarily takes about a month for enough recyclables to accumulate around her house to be worth a trip. Claudia then packs the recyclables on a wagon and walks them down to a redemption center.

This month Claudia was paid a total of $10.64 for the glass and aluminum she turned in. It varies a little from month to month, but according to her log, this month was about $1.50 less than the amount she ordinarily gets for the recyclables, on average. Approximately how much money in recyclables is her family generating per year?

_____

I KNOW I CAN SAVE MONEY!

Claudia has decided to save the money from her recycling efforts. In the past the money has quickly gotten away from her, mostly spent on stuff she did not really need. Claudia has saved the following amounts over the course of four months: $10.35, $9.89, $11.02, $10.54. Claudia plans to buy a savings bond once she has accumulated $50. How much more money does she need in order to buy the bond?

_____

Builder's Creative Idea Catches On

Stanley works as a carpenter, building fine wood cabinets and floors in custom homes. He is always looking to improve his skills and is willing to try new ideas in his work. An idea of Stanley's at a recent job site has proven to be the beginning of a very good side business. Stanley was working on the wood flooring at an old farmhouse when he realized that the boards being replaced were going to be both difficult and expensive to match with new lumber. The property owner mentioned that only the barn and outbuildings had been made with lumber of the same period.

Stanley's idea involved borrowing pieces of wood from one of the outbuildings, then planing this wood to take off the old, weathered surface. The wood could then be used with the flooring project at no cost to the homeowner. The idea proved to be a success, as the owner ended up paying only for Stanley's labor involved in the project. Stanley estimated that buying wood at a specialty wood store would have cost the homeowner $1,850! Stanley worked a total of 31.75 hours on this flooring project, charging $24.50 per hour for his labor. Including Stanley's charge for labor, how much would the homeowner have had to spend on this project if the recycled wood had not been used? _____

Stanley found himself knocking on doors the next week, asking farmers if he could buy the wood from old, decrepit barns and falling-down outbuildings. He spent $2,200 that week buying enough old lumber to completely fill the storage building next to his woodshop.

Stanley used only a small portion of this lumber supply on his next wood project and billed the homeowner $875 for that wood. He figures 80% of the wood he had stockpiled still remained in his storage building. If Stanley is able to bill out the remaining wood at prices similar to what he charged on the first batch, how much will his original investment in wood end up yielding in profit? _____

More About Stanley and His Carpentry Projects

Stanley has just agreed to take on the flooring project in an older house that is being completely renovated inside. The flooring in the living room of this house is in terrible shape and will have to be completely removed. Stanley is planning to use his own lumber for the project, since it has met with a great deal of approval from customers who have seen the finished product. This will also help reduce overall costs for the homeowner.

Stanley measured the living room, finding it to be 24 feet by 16 feet. The homeowner wanted Stanley's price quote for the job to be based on a price per square foot, instead of Stanley's usual cost breakdown of labor and materials. Stanley turned in a quote of $16.50 per square foot. How much was Stanley's price quote for the total living room flooring project? _____

DARN COPYCATS!

Stanley's idea of recycling the wood from old barns and outbuildings has been so successful that other carpenters have started doing the same thing. This has made it more difficult for Stanley to buy his raw materials, since other carpenters are also out looking for old barn wood.

Stanley decided to solve this problem by taking out an advertisement in a local farm magazine. The magazine is published monthly by an electric company cooperative that produces power in rural areas. Stanley thinks that this ad will give him the inside edge for buying lumber. The ad costs $19.99 per month. Stanley paid for his ad to run for one year. How much money did Stanley spend on this new advertising campaign? _____

Hotel Goes to the Dogs

Kay has a large piece of property. She has recently made some significant changes to the property. This included moving fences, building a wider driveway, and converting some outbuildings for different purposes. Part of her strategy for the property renovation is preparing a former horse barn for use as a pet hotel. She plans to rent rooms to the owners of the pets, and then care for their animals while the owners are away.

Kay has taken this old horse barn and improved the lighting, added heat, and set up individual guest rooms in the former stalls. She now wants to run some figures for her new business to see what kind of income she can expect from the pet hotel. The pet hotel has eight rooms, but Kay realizes that they probably will not all be rented continuously. She plans to charge $12 per room, per night. What weekly income can she expect if half the rooms stay rented? _____

Since the pet hotel's opening, Kay has been very busy. Once animals were checked in, Kay found that there was much more to do than she has time for. She has asked a neighbor to help with the daily chores. Kay has offered to give this neighbor a special room rate if she ever needs to use the hotel. The special room rate mentioned was $8 per room, per night. This neighbor has six dogs, but the two smallest dogs get along quite well together and would share a room. What will this neighbor end up paying if she leaves all her dogs at Kay's hotel for 3 nights? _____

WELCOME TO HOTEL FIDO!

More About Kay's Pet Hotel

Business has been good for Kay's Pet Hotel. It has caused her to do some thinking about the rooms. It occurs to her that if the hotel's eight rooms were more luxurious, she could attract a more affluent class of dogs as guests. She could then charge more for the rooms!

Kay is upgrading the hotel's features by replacing the bedding in five of the rooms and installing carpeting in four of the rooms. (The carpeting is a new washable variety.) She will also have an automatic watering system installed in each room to ensure a continuous supply of fresh water for the guests. The bedding will cost $35 per room and the new carpeting will cost $26 per room. The watering systems represent the most expensive improvement, costing $75 per room. How much will all the new improvements cost? _____

THIS PLACE IS THE CAT'S PAJAMAS!

In keeping with her new strategy of improving the hotel's image, Kay has decided to change dog food brands. She wants to find a flashier brand that will appeal to the upscale type of customer she now wishes to attract. Kay found a brand she likes the look of, sold only in veterinarian's offices. The new brand is available only in 25-pound bags, at a cost of $8.89 per bag. In contrast, the old dog food cost $14.49 for a 50-pound bag. How much more will she pay for the new dog food each time 50 pounds is used?

_____

Power Outage Prompts Low-Tech Solution

Clark works for Medi-Fill, a large chain of retail drug stores. He is quite impressed by the computerized inventory system at the store where he works. Inventory needs are handled automatically, since the store's high-tech cash registers are linked automatically with the warehouse distribution center. The cash registers are programmed to automatically take into account product discounts and to compute the sales tax on purchases. Managers have told Clark that it is almost impossible to make a mistake when using these registers.

One evening, Clark was working when a thunderstorm moved through the area and knocked out electrical power to the store. Even though the cash register could not be used, Clark decided that he would tally customer purchases by hand and enter them into the register later when the power came back on. If the tax rate on prescription medicine is 2%, how much sales tax should Clark collect on an $18 prescription medicine purchase? _____

Clark recently stopped by a newsstand located near his apartment building. He likes to drop in there occasionally after work to see if there is anything that looks interesting to read. Clark is particularly interested in financial news, since he hopes to start his own business some day. On this occasion, Clark purchased a newspaper for $2.55 and a $4.95 magazine. He knows that the sales tax on printed material is 4%. Clark was charged a total of $.40 for sales tax on his purchases. But he did not realize a mistake had been made until after he had already gotten home. How much money was Clark overcharged for sales tax on this purchase?

_____

THIS PAGE IS TAXING!

Book Exchange Policy Baffles Patron

Bruce owns the Paperback Exchange Book Store. Most of Bruce's business is built around people trading used paperbacks at a set ratio of exchange and paying a small cash fee for the exchange. Bruce also has a fair number of customers who just buy books for cash and have no trades to make.

Bruce always dreads visits to his store by Mrs. Whipple. He has explained to her a number of times that she may trade in books at a ratio of 3 for 1. In other words, three of her trade-in books equal one book from the store's inventory. Then a charge of 25 cents is added for each book she selects from the store's inventory. Bruce has explained this to her a number of times, but he inevitably has to go through it all over again every visit. This visit, Mrs. Whipple has brought 12 books to trade. How many of the store's books may she select in trade for the number of books she has brought in?

_____

Bruce keeps a small selection of hardcover books in his store. These are mostly nonfiction titles in the areas of history, art, architecture, cooking, health, and local interest. Bruce has no trading policy on these books. If he can use the books in the store, he pays ¼ of the listed retail price for them whenever someone brings them in. Bruce then sells these books at ½ of the listed retail price. Bruce is buying the following books from a customer with retail prices noted: *Architecture of the South* $24.00, *French Cooking with Wine* $18.65, *Treasury of American Coins* $60.00, and *Design Your Own Circulating Water Fountain* $12.95. If Bruce buys these books under his normal policy, how much will he owe this customer for the books?

_____

Name _____

A Well-Numbered Garden

Teresa keeps a large garden. This has been her main interest for a number of years. She routinely collects data about her garden in an attempt to better understand the growth process of the plants. Often, she treats different groups of plants with varying amounts of fertilizer and water to see which combination produces the best results. She recently measured the heights of 16 sunflowers she had grown in four different controlled plots. The shortest sunflower was 54 centimeters. The tallest sunflower in the group was 81 centimeters. She did not like the tallest sunflower, as the stalk was too thin to support the flower once it had matured. The shorter sunflower lacked height, but Teresa was still impressed by its supportive stalk and healthier-looking flower. How many centimeters in height separated the two sunflowers? _____

Teresa is concerned that a hot, dry pattern seems to have settled in for the summer. Rain has been very scarce during this period, so Teresa has been using an automatic sprinkler system for her garden. She would ordinarily run the sprinkler for 25 minutes in the mornings, just long enough to lightly water the plants. This was usually an adequate amount of time. But with the weather so hot and dry, her garden was beginning to suffer. Teresa reprogrammed her sprinkler system to run for 20 minutes in the morning and then another 20 minutes in the late afternoon. The sprinkler system delivers 13 liters of water per minute to the plants. How much water is now being distributed to the garden daily by the sprinkler system?

_____

More About Teresa's Garden

Teresa's flowers are the envy of her neighborhood. She has on occasion even won awards at flower shows. She grows a number of different flower varieties but seems to have a knack for producing fine marigolds. Teresa planted extra marigolds at the start of the spring and now has 200 extra seedlings in her greenhouse. She plans to give her sister 50 of those marigolds. The rest of the seedlings will be split equally among five neighbors who have helped her with gardening chores from time to time. How many marigold seedlings will each of these neighbors receive? _____

GROW, BABY, GROW!

Teresa is making some changes to her garden. This includes treatments for the soil and improvements to the overall drainage system in the garden. Teresa had the following items delivered: 400 kilograms of fertilizer, 250 kilograms of a special potting soil, 1,225 kilograms of large drainage rock, 300 kilograms of pea gravel, and 525 kilograms of lime. She had no way of transporting these items herself and instead chose to pay for delivery. The delivery charge was $6 per 100 kilograms of weight, regardless of the material involved. Teresa was also charged $20 for each truck that had to be dispatched to her property. Everything was put on a single truck except for the drainage rock, which required a second truck. What was her total charge for all the deliveries?

_____

Film Editing— A Matter of Time

Kit recently joined a production company that specializes in producing both educational and hobby-related films and videos. Kit's main assignment is editing films, although she may be asked to help with other projects from time to time. One of Kit's first tasks is reworking a documentary.

The film chronicles the restoration efforts of a local group as it renovated a historic house near the city's waterfront. Kit has been given 3 hours and 20 minutes of raw footage, shot by a film crew at the house renovation site. The raw footage represents unedited film, only some of which will be useable. Kit has been told to create a 48-minute film, using whatever portions of the raw footage she thinks best. How much of the raw footage will not be used for creating this 48-minute film? _____

Kit has been working on a series titled *Crafts of the Appalachian Mountains*. Once finished, the series will be sold as a set of four tapes. Each tape in the series will be 80 minutes in length. Pottery making, basket weaving, woodworking, and gardening will be the main topics covered by the *Crafts of the Appalachian Mountains* series.

Kit has been looking at the footage shot by film crews for the craft series. She is quite pleased with most of it so far. Over 9 hours of raw footage was shot for the segment on pottery making alone! However, Kit is concerned that the 3 hours and 10 minutes of footage shot for the gardening segment is cutting things a bit close. It will not leave her very much extra material to work with when editing the gardening segment. Kit does expect to have enough raw film to produce all the planned programs. Once the project is completed, how long will the total run time be for *Crafts of the Appalachian Mountains*? _____

More About Kit's Film Editing Work

Kit was asked to look at a series of tapes edited by a former employee of the company. This particular series is titled *The Secrets of Fish*. The series is composed of three tapes. Each tape is 45 minutes in length. The series was created to document little-known facts about the behavior and life cycles of fish, but, unfortunately, the series generated a lot of complaints from people who bought it. The word *boring* seemed to pop up frequently among the complaints sent in. A few people also were disappointed that the tapes were not about fishing, as they had mistakenly thought when they purchased them.

Kit has some ideas for improving *The Secrets of Fish* series. First, she will change the title to *The Secret Lives of Fish*. This should eliminate the confusion over whether they are programs about fishing. Next, she plans to reduce the series to just two tapes, each one hour long. This should eliminate some of the segments that people thought were boring. How many minutes of material will Kit be removing from the series?

_____

Kit has been assigned the task of editing a documentary on the weather of the New England coastal areas. The raw footage for this project was shot a few years ago, then set aside due to budgetary concerns. Kit's supervisor now wants her to look at the material that is on tape and decide what length film could most sensibly be produced from it. Kit thinks that the topic would be well served by a single 40-minute program, but she has not made up her mind.

Kit pulled the eight tapes involved in the weather project from the company's film library. Each tape contains 45 minutes of raw footage. Kit wants to look at all of the material before deciding how to proceed with the project. How many hours of material must she now screen? _____

Bread Making Takes Planning

Ellie is going to try a bread recipe sent to her by her grandmother. She is having friends over for a get-together and wants to serve homemade bread as part of the dinner. In looking at her grandmother's recipe, it appears to make only two loaves of bread. Ellie thinks that she will need five loaves of bread for her company.

Ellie realizes that she will have to adjust all the quantities shown in her grandmother's recipe to provide for the extra loaves needed. What multiplier should Ellie use for each of the recipe items to yield the proper amount of dough? _____

Ellie's next obstacle with the bread recipe involved the preparation time. Her grandmother had jotted down the amount of time needed for each stage of the recipe in the margin. But the amount had not been totaled. Ellie needs to determine the length of time needed for the entire recipe so that she knows how far in advance the bread should be prepared.

Mixing the ingredients and kneading the dough was listed in the recipe as taking 25 minutes. Allowing the bread to rise was listed as taking 40 minutes. Kneading the dough a second time and separating it into loaves was shown as taking 12 minutes. Letting the dough rise a final time was listed as taking 45 minutes. Baking time was given as being precisely 22 minutes. How much time from start to finish does it take to prepare bread according to this recipe? _____

Preparing Aquarium Requires Study

Chloe has been saving her money to buy a saltwater aquarium. She has managed to accumulate $825, probably just enough to get started with her new hobby. Chloe has also been studying all the complexities involved in setting up a saltwater aquarium. From what she has read, Chloe thinks much more will be required for getting a saltwater aquarium up and running than the tropical fish aquariums she is used to keeping.

Chloe has been pricing items she will need. The aquarium itself will cost $329.99, and its table, $150. A suitable filter system will run $129.99. Chloe will also need to buy crushed coral and other supplies for the interior of the tank at a cost of $79.99. A chemical kit, $49.50, will be needed to properly condition the water. After Chloe has bought all these items, how much of her aquarium fund will remain for buying the fish? _____

In studying saltwater aquariums, Chloe read that no more than eight fish should be kept per 100 gallons of aquarium size. She thinks that recommendation may be a bit on the low side, but Chloe plans to follow it until she has had more experience with her new saltwater aquarium. If her new aquarium is a 150-gallon model, what is the maximum number of fish Chloe should keep? _____

Hobbyist Takes Train Models Too Far

Bo's hobby is collecting model trains and building layouts for them. This is what Bo does with all his spare time. It is also what he does with all his spare money! Bo has been working on a complicated track layout for about four months. He has spent nearly $200 getting the layout ready for the train he plans to run. This figure would be much higher, except for the fact that Bo creates many things for his layouts that other people ordinarily just buy for theirs. People who know Bo think he is obsessive in this regard, but Bo's wife says that it keeps him busy.

With the layout nearly complete, Bo has turned his attention to buying the engine, boxcars, and caboose he wants for his layout. Bo still has $325 in his train fund set aside to purchase this train. He knows that the engine alone will cost $149.99, and the caboose will cost $79.99. Those are the items he will buy first. He will then use the rest of the money in his train fund to buy boxcars at a cost of $39.99 each. How many boxcars will Bo be able to purchase with the funds remaining after the engine and caboose are purchased? _____

Bo is a member of a train collectors group. The group meets once a month at a local pancake house to discuss new products, price trends, upcoming train events, and other hobby-related issues. One of the members of the group has been pestering Bo to sell him a special commemorative-edition engine he owns. This collector has offered Bo $400 for this engine, representing a very reasonable figure for the engine involved.

Bo is considering the offer, but he would rather sell the family dog than part with a train. (This particular engine is not even one of Bo's favorites.) Bo recalls buying the train by mail order a few years back for $189.95 and paying a $20.50 shipping fee. How much profit would Bo make if he sold the commemorative engine to this eager collector? _____

More About Bo's Train Hobby

Bo has been working on the most complicated train layout he has ever designed. He thinks that this will be *the* layout that earns him the centerfold in Train Hobbyist Monthly Magazine. Bo will set up this layout in his mother-in-law's old bedroom. She used to live with Bo and his wife but her leg is almost healed, so Bo sent her back to her own home. Relatives think that Bo has gone too far, kicking someone out of the house just to use her space for trains. But Bo thinks that a person who is truly committed to important hobby goals should not be sidetracked simply by family issues.

Bo will use the entire room for this layout. The room is 12 feet by 12 feet. Bo will build a tabletop covering this entire area, except for a narrow center aisle 3 feet wide and 6 feet long which will allow worthy people to enter the room and view the layout. Bo has planned this layout down to the square inch. How many square inches does he have to work with in his layout? _____

Bo finally had to seek professional help with regard to his hobby. His employer at the paint store where Bo works insisted. This came after Bo kept asking customers in line to have tickets ready for boarding. Earlier that same day Bo yelled "all aboard!" at a woman who asked if he could match a paint sample for her.

ALL ABOARD!

Bo found a doctor he likes, but his therapy sessions are only 60% covered by his insurance carrier. Bo's doctor ordinarily charges $200 per session but has arranged to charge Bo only $120 per session since he agreed to be the subject of a journal article the doctor is planning to write. How much money does Bo pay out-of-pocket per session with his doctor since the insurance carrier will not cover the full amount? _____

Not Turning Limes into Limeade

Betty has a small lime orchard in her backyard. Every year, the trees produce large, attractive fruit. While the limes are quite nice to look at, they are a variety that is too sour to eat. Betty has tried mixing the lime juice with sugar water to make limeade, but the limes are too strong even for that. One day, Betty was watching a program on television about the popularity of natural and chemical-free products. She looked outside the window at her lime trees. They were laden with useless fruit. An idea suddenly came to her about what to do with her limes.

The first step was harvesting the limes. Betty selected a tree of average size that appeared to have a good quantity of fruit. She timed herself in picking the limes on this tree, since she felt that it would be representative of the time needed to finish each of the 19 other trees in her little orchard. It took Betty 1 hour and 40 minutes to get all the limes off this tree and into boxes in her garage. How long will it take her to harvest the entire orchard if the time spent on this single tree turns out to be a good representative average of the time needed for harvesting each of the other trees?

_____

Betty has finally finished the lime harvest. She also has purchased a commercial citrus fruit squeezer at a cost of $149.99. Betty will squeeze all the limes and collect the juice in empty plastic milk jugs that she has been saving. Betty intends to mix the lime juice with vinegar and water to make an all-purpose household cleaning fluid. She has already tried out her secret formula in her own kitchen and bathroom with good results. It even seems to work exceptionally well cleaning windows, leaving behind no terrible chemical smell.

Betty still needs to buy a quantity of vinegar and a sufficient supply of empty plastic spray bottles. Betty has found out that the vinegar will cost $48.50 and the quantity of empty spray bottles needed will cost $169. By the time these items are purchased, how much will Betty have spent so far in getting this idea off the ground? _____

More About Betty and Her Product Idea

Once Betty had the chance to assemble all the necessary supplies, she began making her cleaning solution according to her secret formula. The formula she was using was essentially a 3:1 ratio. It involved three parts lime juice to one part vinegar. Betty first poured 6 ounces of lime juice into an empty plastic spray bottle. She then added the correct amount of vinegar. Betty then topped off each bottle with water, twisted on the spray cap, and shook the bottle to mix the ingredients. She repeated this process until all the bottles were properly filled. How much vinegar was put into each spray bottle before the water was added? _____

It took several days, but Betty finally finished filling all the plastic spray bottles with her secret lime-based cleaning formula. She first began showing the product around to friends and neighbors, looking for feedback on how well they liked it. Betty was sufficiently encouraged by their comments to rent a booth at an upcoming home-and-garden show.

The home-and-garden show turned out to be a huge success for Betty. The aisles were clogged with people, and Betty had many people stop to watch her product demonstrations. She conducted these demonstrations all day and managed to sell 421 bottles of her cleaning solution by the end of the day. She was left with very little inventory at the end of the day, which made her think of expanding her business beyond what her own small lime orchard could produce. How much money did Betty take in at the home-and-garden show if she priced her lime-based cleaning product at $2.89 per bottle? _____

Computer Deal Not What It Seems

Jake has been shopping for a computer. He has looked at a number of different brands, considering both mail-order companies as well as local stores that carry computers. Jake is somewhat confused by all the different deals he has seen offered. Some computers are sold at what seems like tremendous discounts, but the purchaser must agree to use a particular Internet service provider for a set time period. Other computers seem more expensive but have no obligation in terms of Internet carriers.

Jake has narrowed his choices to either Computer A, which costs $899 and carries no obligation to use a particular Internet service provider; or Computer B, which costs only $599 but requires the purchaser to sign up for 2 years with a specific Internet service provider at a cost of $24.95 per month. How much more money does Jake obligate himself to spending if he goes with Computer B instead of Computer A?

_____

Jake eventually decided to go with a more expensive computer system, which came with no Internet service provider obligation. He shopped for an Internet service provider which best suited his own needs and found a local service that offers unlimited access for $9.95 per month. How much will Jake spend for this Internet service if he chooses to use it for 2 years?

_____

Name _____

Land Buyer Knows Needs

Vera is planning to buy a small piece of land. She has been out several times with a real-estate agent to look at potential properties. Vera owns three horses which she currently pays to board at a stable near town. Vera would like to buy a suitable piece of land out in the country for her horses and eventually build a small horse barn there. Having her own piece of land would save her the $75 per month per horse fee she is currently paying to keep her horses at the stable.

Vera thinks that each horse should have an average of 2¾ acres to avoid wearing out the pasture and turning it into a mud lot. If she follows the limit she has set, what is the smallest piece of land she should consider buying for her horses? _____

Vera has found a nice piece of property with a small creek running through it. The land is all fenced pasture with an old horse barn already on the property. The 12 acres are more land than she initially wanted, but the setting is too ideal for Vera to pass up. She has often dreamed of having a place like this for her horses and the extra land would enable her to have other animals as well. Vera plans to eventually build a house on the property since there is so much room.

Vera has made the owner an offer of $42,600 for the property. If her offer is accepted, how much money per acre will she be paying for the land? _____

Recycling Center Watches Pennies

The Use-It-Again Recycling Center was formerly called Eddie's Junk Center. Eddie has stopped taking in any sort of merchandise and now concentrates only on plastics, metals, cardboard, paper, and other items with a clearly recyclable potential. Eddie has found markets for all the materials he now accepts. This keeps inventories moving and cash flowing. People living near the Use-It-Again Recycling Center say that the neighborhood also smells better since Eddie gave up the junk business.

Friday is the day most of Eddie's materials are picked up by the companies who buy what he has accumulated during the week. On Friday Eddie sold 400 pounds of cardboard at a profit of $.12 per pound. He sold 335 pounds of aluminum at a profit of $.16 per pound. He also sold 160 pounds of copper at a profit of $.21 per pound. How much profit did Eddie make on these sales? _____

Eddie charges people fees to drop off certain kinds of materials. Batteries are one such item. Eddie is able to sell the batteries, but he receives so little for them that he must charge when the batteries are dropped off in order to make handling them worthwhile. Eddie charges $.15 per pound for batteries dropped off at Use-It-Again Recycling Center. On Thursday only two customers brought in batteries to drop off. One customer had 127 pounds of old automobile batteries. The other customer had 16 pounds of dead household batteries. How much money did Eddie make on Thursday from these batteries? _____

More About Use-It-Again Recycling Center

Eddie has done so well with his new recycling business that he is considering expanding into liquid recyclables. Eddie will soon begin collecting used cooking oil at Use-It-Again Recycling Center. He has contacted a number of fast-food restaurants in the area, all quite eager to get rid of their used oil. First, Eddie needs to purchase 24 plastic drums to collect the oil when it is brought in. Each drum will hold 30 gallons of oil. He also plans to buy 40 plastic jugs that will hold 2 gallons of oil each. How much total oil storage capacity will these purchases allow? _____

Eddie has received an inquiry from a large factory that completely refurbished its entire plumbing system. The factory replaced all copper piping with new plastic piping. Eddie has been asked to pick up the 2,300 pounds of copper piping leftover after the job was completed. The copper is being offered to him free of charge; he just has to pick it up. Eddie has a problem though. His truck is in the shop having repair work done to the transmission. Eddie has decided to use his van to pick up the scrap copper, since this is an opportunity too good to miss. He knows from experience that he can move only about 450 pounds of the awkward and bulky pipes per trip. How many trips will he have to make to the factory to remove all the copper piping? _____

Outdoor Projects Depend on Accuracy

Sergio is helping his father measure their yard. The two have a number of outdoor projects planned for the yard. Sergio knows that having accurate measurements is important for these kinds of projects. Their property is shaped like a large rectangle. The yard's longer sides measure 180 feet. The shorter sides of the yard are 160 feet long.

Sergio and his father will be installing a fence to keep the family dog from roaming and Sergio's younger brother from getting out into the street. The two have been pricing fence material, and Sergio's father thinks that the fence can be built for $1.90 per foot. If this figure is correct, how much will it cost to fully enclose their yard with a fence? _____

Sergio measured their backyard as being 160 feet by 80 feet. The lawn in the backyard is quite thin in spots from heavy play and needs to be reseeded. Sergio's father has told him that the backyard lawn project would be his responsibility. Since part of his allowance is riding on the success of the project, Sergio has taken it quite seriously.

Sergio began by reading the planting instructions printed on the bags of grass seed at the home improvement store. The brand he intends to use lists one 20-pound bag as sufficient for planting or replanting 1,500 square feet of lawn area. If Sergio follows the company's recommendation, how many 20-pound bags of grass seed will need to be bought for their backyard lawn? _____

More About Sergio's Projects

Sergio's dad assigned him another task since Sergio did so well with the others. An outdoor storage box is needed for storing small garden tools, coiled garden hoses, empty flowerpots, and other outdoor items they want to keep out of sight. The only requirement Sergio's dad put on the project was that the box should have at least 16 cubic feet of interior storage space.

Sergio has decided to make the storage box look like an outdoor bench so that it serves a dual purpose. The storage box will be used on the patio to supplement their outdoor seating. Sergio plans to make the interior length of the storage box 48 inches and the width 18 inches. What is the minimum height Sergio must make the interior of the box to meet his father's storage space requirement? _____

IF YOU BUILD IT THEY WILL PAY!

Sergio did a fine job with his storage box/bench project. Everyone who sees it is impressed with the functional design and finished look of the box. After seeing the storage bench, a neighbor even asked Sergio to build an identical bench for his outdoor patio.

Sergio agreed to build the bench, but he was unsure what to charge. Since his father had paid for all the materials involved, Sergio had no idea what to charge for them. The neighbor told Sergio that he would pay for the materials if given a list and would then just pay Sergio for his time. The price agreed upon for the project was $30. How much will Sergio make per hour if the storage box/bench can be built in just 1 hour, 40 minutes?

_____

Name _____

Poll Surprises Student

Elaine is doing a statistics project as part of a school math course. Her project will involve polling people at random as they enter the school. She will select people at random so that she does not poll only people she knows. The random factor in her poll will lead to better results, since Elaine has no idea in advance what these students will say. Elaine plans to ask 50 people this simple question: "Should the school board pay for insurance for the school's football program next year?" This question has become a topic of debate in the community, and Elaine thinks that it would make a fine polling question for her project.

Elaine conducted her poll on a recent morning before school opened. Twenty-nine people said "No" or a similar response meaning no, such as "No way." Eleven people said "Yes" or a response meaning yes. Four people said "Don't Know," which Elaine put into a category marked as such. The remaining people's responses fell into a category she marked "Other Response." This category included comments such as "Don't bother me with this kind of garbage!" or "Are you some kind of nut?" What percentage of people gave responses that fell in the "Other Response" category? _____

The results of her first poll surprised Elaine so much that she decided to conduct the poll again to see if the results would be similar. She asked the same question of another 50 people at random and got the following results: No–31, Yes–9, Don't Know–8, Other Response–2. Elaine decided that the results of this poll were very similar to the last poll. In this latest poll, what percentage of people favored the school board paying for insurance for the football program? _____

HMM...

Math Means Money to Home Owner

Collin is planning to sell his house. He has had the place for several years but will soon move to another state and plans to sell the property. Collin has put quite a bit of research into the housing market in his area. From studying recent sales in his neighborhood, Collin thinks his house is worth $144,000.

Collin still owes $92,554 on his house in the form of a mortgage held by First City Bank. That loan will have to be paid off in full when the house goes to closing. The realtor will collect a fee of 6% on the sale price of the house, also to be paid at closing. Collin will have to pay other closing-related fees amounting to $3,255. If Collin is able to sell his house for what he thinks it's worth, how much money will be left over from the sale after the mortgage is paid off and the other fees and commissions are settled? _____

Collin changed his mind about selling his house himself. He plans to rent it instead. The house should easily rent for $1,375 per month. Collin has decided to retain a real-estate management company to handle showing the property and collecting the rent.

After interviewing several realty management companies, Collin decided to go with Cross Town Real Estate. Their advertising program was the single most important factor distinguishing this firm from the numerous other real-estate management firms in the area. Cross Town Real Estate charges a 10% commission on monthly rentals collected on behalf of the property owner. After paying this fee, how much money will Collin have left each month if his own mortgage payment on the property is $955 per month?

_____

Warehouse Owner Looks to Grow Business

Bernhard owns Safe Storage Warehouse and Transfer. The warehouse facility occupies a choice location, not far from the city's port district. Bernhard has guided the business along very carefully, specializing in short-term storage of crates and container boxes. Bernhard discourages his staff from allowing freight to be left longer than a week. He also frowns on storing smaller parcels that are difficult to inventory and track. Bernhard has a vision of how money is made in the warehouse business and he does not like to stray from that plan.

Bernhard has just arranged to store 50 crates for one of his regular customers. Each crate has a width of 4 feet and a length of 4 feet. The crates are all 6 feet tall and must be stored upright. As per the shipper's instructions, the crates may have nothing stacked on top of them. How many total feet of floor space will the crates occupy while they are being stored at Safe Storage? _____

Bernhard is building a second warehouse facility to handle the business he is now forced to turn away during peak shipping periods. The facility is costing him a fortune to construct, over two million dollars by the time it is finished! But Bernhard is confident that the business will prove to be quite lucrative for the extra warehouse, especially once the nearby port begins to receive additional shipping traffic. The new warehouse is immense. Its interior dimensions will be 400 feet wide by 600 feet long once it is completed. The interior height will be 20 feet. How many cubic feet of storage space will be available in this warehouse when construction is completed? _____

YEAH MAN!

More About Safe Storage Warehouse

Bernhard is reviewing his security procedures. Valuable goods are stored in his care each night, and Bernhard is responsible for those goods. Any losses would not only hurt profits, but his reputation as well. That is why Bernhard is having a new security system installed. The new security system will serve as a backup to the on-site security guards he already employs.

The new security system is comprised of a series of cameras that will be tied to a panel of closed-circuit televisions. An employee will monitor these images from a remote location. Bernhard is paying $24,000 for the new security system. This price includes installation. He is also paying a monthly fee of $225 for monitoring and maintenance. What will Bernhard's total cost be for the new security system during the first year? _____

Bernhard is contemplating a buy-out offer he has received for Safe Storage Warehouse and Transfer. On the surface the offer seems reasonable to Bernhard. He is familiar with every aspect of his warehouse business, and the offer seems to fairly address that. However, Bernhard is suspicious that the buyers might be after the land itself, rather than the shipping business. That is why he has called three real-estate agents out to provide him with new appraisals.

The first realtor prepared a list of similar properties around the city and gave Bernhard a figure of $4,340,000. The second agent thought that the property would be worth five million dollars to a retail developer, especially when compared to other available properties. The last agent saw no potential for anything other than a warehouse business, turning in an appraisal of only $2,900,000. Bernhard will take the average of all the estimates and use that figure in his calculations. What figure did Bernhard arrive at for the value of the land? _____

Paperwork Makes Fieldwork Go More Smoothly

Tom is a partner at the Landscape Designs Unlimited firm. The firm produces landscape ideas and layouts for both homeowners and commercial property owners. Landscape Designs Unlimited does most of the design work on computers. Tom handles a number of projects through his office each week. Tom's specialty is presenting project ideas to the firm's fussier clients. Even though the firm is heavily geared toward computerized design, Tom does most of his layout work by hand. He produces drawings for clients who are hard to please and not impressed by computer-generated layouts.

Tom has been working on a design job for a residential customer. He worked 6 hours on this job Monday and completed the job after spending another 5.5 hours on it Tuesday. Tom's time is billed at $27.50 per hour. How much will the client owe for this design job? _____

Tom has taken on a small but difficult project for a client living in the city. The client owns a townhouse in a very fashionable area of town. But the townhouse has a backyard that is very small. The dimensions of the yard are 18 feet by 24 feet, and a small patio consumes a portion of that space. The owner wants a privacy fence installed enclosing the entire back yard along the property lines. If the house itself forms the border of one of the 24-foot sides of the backyard, how many feet of privacy fence will Tom need to plan in his drawing? _____

84

More About Landscape Designs Unlimited

Landscape Designs Unlimited produces plans and layout designs for landscaping projects, but the firm does not perform the actual landscaping work. Tom will arrange and manage the landscaping work if the client prefers. When this occurs, Landscape Designs Unlimited pays the landscapers involved and considers this amount when computing the client's total bill. Tom has several landscapers he uses on a regular basis for this type of work. He has arranged a meeting with one of his regular landscapers to estimate the work involved with a design he has developed for a client.

The landscaper will perform the work according to Tom's design for $2,200. The project estimate calls for approximately 50 hours labor. A standard clause in the contract allows the landscaper to charge up to an additional 15% for cost of labor overruns. Tom plans to charge the client a total of $45,000 for the completed landscaping project. What is the least amount of profit Landscape Designs Unlimited will make on this project if labor cost overruns are added? _____

QUALITY FRUIT COSTS BIG BUCKS!

Tom has taken on a challenging project. He will be responsible for designing a 16-acre flower garden and fruit orchard for an important client of the firm. This represents the largest piece of property Tom has ever prepared a landscape plan for. He has a lot of creative ideas for utilizing the property's many natural features, but one item has given him cause for concern. He noticed in the project budget that only $4,000 had been allocated for the purchase of trees. Tom knows that the cost of a quality fruit tree of a size that is useable for this project is $115 per tree. Planting trees of this size will cost $45 each, and supplying each tree with a sufficient irrigation system is another $25 per tree. If the tree budget remains unchanged, how many trees will it allow Tom to include in his plan? _____

Deals Lacking at Wholesale Club?

Kerrie is considering joining Big Savings Wholesale Club. She has heard from a number of her friends that the club is a place of countless bargains, available only to members. Kerrie is skeptical but wants to check the facts for herself.

Kerrie is visiting Big Savings Wholesale Club with a friend who is already a member. She wants to spot check a few items before joining the club to see if the savings are really there. Kerrie noticed that a 1-gallon jar of mayonnaise costs $6.50 at Big Savings Wholesale Club. The mayonnaise is not even her favorite brand, and storing such a quantity in the refrigerator would be cumbersome. Kerrie is not even sure how many years it would take to use that much mayonnaise, but it would likely spoil before it was all used. Kerrie currently pays $1.99 per quart for her favorite brand of mayonnaise at her regular supermarket. How much would it cost Kerrie to buy an equivalent amount of her favorite brand of mayonnaise at her regular supermarket? _____

Kerrie admits that there would be a slight savings for her on some products offered by Big Savings Wholesale Club. But she is still not convinced that membership in Big Savings Wholesale Club is right for her. She has no real need for gallon jars of mayonnaise, 10-pound boxes of cookies, or oil drum-sized containers of laundry detergent.

The club charges $75 per year for a membership. Since her regular supermarket charges nothing for her to shop there, Kerrie thinks that the club fee may be too high to be worthwhile. She cannot see herself shopping at the club more than a half-dozen times a year. If her estimate proved to be correct, how much would each trip to the club have cost her on average? _____

Medication Schedule Worries Caregiver

Malorie is occasionally asked to look after her grandfather. He is not really much trouble, since he reads or watches television most of the day. But a family member must be around the house whenever the day nurse is gone in case he has a medical emergency.

Malorie worries about her grandfather's medication schedule. He takes so many different prescription drugs each day that a chart is needed for keeping up with them. A space on this chart must be checked off as each dose is given. Her grandfather takes four doses of a high blood pressure medication each day. He must also have his heart medicine six times a day. He also takes a pill for arthritis twice a day and another medicine once a day that controls his cholesterol level. He also takes a medicine to assist with liver functioning in the morning and again in the evening. How many doses of medicine does Malorie's grandfather need to take each day? _____

Malorie took a reading for her grandfather's blood pressure at 7 a.m. and made a note of the figure for when the nurse returns. They monitor her grandfather's blood pressure to make certain that his medications are working as expected.

Malorie's grandfather is supposed to have his blood pressure checked every four and a half hours during the day. At what time should his first afternoon blood pressure reading be taken? _____

Pet Grooming Goes Upscale

Marcie owns Pet Fashions Grooming and Accessories Store. Her main business is built around shampooing dogs, but she also carries a selection of doggie sweaters and clothing items in the store. Marcie recently received $1,400 after her accountant amended a previous tax return. She plans to reinvest all of this money in the store.

Marcie is going to use $595 of the money to buy a self-serve cappuccino machine for the customer waiting area. She thinks that the cappuccino machine will give customers a reason to stay in the store, instead of just dropping off their animals. Marcie is certain that more sweaters and other doggie accessories will be sold if customers can be tempted to wait in the store while their pets are being groomed. Marcie will use the rest of the tax refund to buy doggie sweaters at a cost of $12.25 each. This is a good deal for Marcie, since she sells the sweaters for $19.99 retail price. How many sweaters will Marcie be able to buy with the money remaining after the cappuccino machine is purchased? _____

Marcie became a bit distracted one day while talking to a customer on the telephone. She was also trying to groom an expensive poodle at the same time. Unfortunately, the shears cut off too much of the dog's hair. Although unhurt, the dog looked like it had been prepped for surgery. The dog's owner was greatly upset by the mistake and threatened to sue Pet Fashions Grooming and Accessories Store!

Marcie immediately offered to tear up the customer's $24.95 bill for the dog's grooming, and she also offered to do the dog's next shampoo and flea dip free of charge, normally an $18.95 value. This seemed to have the desired effect on the dog's angry owner. The customer made an appointment for the following week to have the free shampooing done and also apologized for the lawsuit threats. How much money in fees did Marcie give up in order to placate the angry poodle owner? _____

More About Pet Fashions Store

Business has been rather slow at Pet Fashions Grooming and Accessories Store. Marcie hopes to stimulate interest by running a series of advertisements in the local newspaper. She wants to remind potential customers of the benefits of having a clean, well-groomed dog around the house. She also wants to remind people of her wide selection of pet accessories and related products.

Marcie has been evaluating the newspaper's pricing policy for publishing advertisements. The cost of advertising declines as more ads are run. Marcie has agreed to run a ⅛-page ad in the next 12 issues of the newspaper. This ad will cost $44 per insertion. How much money has Marcie committed to this ad campaign? _____

THESE DOLLARS MAKE SENSE!

Marcie loaned one of her employees $375 to use for travel and entry expenses related to a dog show. The employee had previously won a few local events, and Marcie figured that it would be good publicity for the store if the dogs won anything at the regional competition. The employee's dogs did not win any of the show events, but a lot of people did ask about their care and grooming.

Marcie has agreed to let the employee pay $25 per week until the loan has been repaid. No interest will be charged for this loan. How many weeks will it take for the loan to be paid back if no payments are missed? _____

Treasure Hunter Finds Fortune

Gregory's hobby is looking for buried treasure. He has a metal detector and uses it to look for lost (or long-hidden) items. Gregory has found a number of coins and rings while out using his metal detector, but all have been of very modest value. He has also found lots of bottle caps, scraps of tin foil, nails, cans, and other junk.

Gregory always hopes to strike it rich with his metal detector, but he is usually lucky to find enough coins to pay for his machine's batteries. His metal detector uses eight AA-size batteries and a single nine-volt battery. Gregory replaces all the batteries at once, buying 2 four-packs at a cost of $3.99 each. The nine-volt battery costs $1.89. How much does it cost Gregory to put a full set of new batteries in his metal detector? _____

On a recent outing, Gregory had the opportunity to explore a relative's property. The property was vacant but had once been the site of a very old farmhouse, barn, and outbuildings. After much searching, the day was beginning to look like a waste of effort until Gregory unearthed a small tin box. The box had to be opened with his digging tool since it was rusted shut.

Far from being a treasure box, the stuff inside looked like keepsakes to Gregory. It appeared to be all paper items, clippings, and things a person might keep in a scrapbook, not a buried box. On top of the small pile was a booklet titled *Madame Olga Reveals Your Fortune*. It was an advertising booklet for a fortune-teller. Inside the booklet were several predictions and a calendar for the year 1927. A theater ticket was dated 1939. An envelope carried a postmark from 1936. Gregory looked through the rest of the box and could find nothing else dated except the invitation for a high school commencement in 1933. These dates appeared to be the only clues as to how long these items had been accumulated by whomever had buried them. What date was lacking in the collection for having a completed pattern spanning the years between 1927 and 1939? _____

More About Gregory and His Hobby

Gregory has been thinking about his metal-detecting hobby and all the time he spends on it. Gregory figures that he spends about 4 hours per week on this hobby, having done that pretty consistently over the course of the past 2 years. This figure represents his best estimate, not an exact figure. Gregory wonders if he might have been wiser to use his time reading, learning about computers, or practicing art. If Gregory's estimate is correct, how much time has he spent on his metal detecting hobby during the past 2 years? _____

Gregory finally had a lucky day at the beach with his metal detector. Winter ordinarily draws few people to the beach, and Gregory had the place all to himself. He likes this kind of day since it is quiet, and he does not have to deal with people asking him questions about what he is doing and if he has found anything. Conditions seemed advantageous as well. A storm had just passed through the area the day before. Gregory had heard that this increases the possibility of waves pushing good items ashore.

Gregory was sweeping an area with his detector about 100 feet from the water, just where the high surf had crested the night before during the storm. A clear, strong

signal gave him cause for hope. Gregory was delighted when the signal turned out to be a solid gold ring with a large green emerald mounted in the center. Gregory thought the ring had an antique look about it, a fact later verified by the jeweler who appraised it. The ring had an appraised value of $10,000, but the jeweler thought that it could reasonably be expected to sell for $8,500 at auction. This sounded great to Gregory! How much money separated the ring's appraised value from the amount the jeweler thought it would bring at auction?

_____

Nearsighted Customer Looks at Eyeglass Choices

Brenda recently went in for an eye exam and found that her glasses needed changing. Brenda is nearsighted, so seeing distant things is difficult when not wearing her eyeglasses.

Brenda always gets her eyeglasses at Ready in an Hour Eyeglasses Shop. She does not use the shop for their one-hour service, since that applies to only one style of frames. But the shop does have a price special that she thinks is quite fair. Ready in an Hour offers a second pair of glasses at ½ price when buying one pair at regular price. Brenda has selected a pair of glasses that costs $146.50. How much money will Brenda be spending on eyeglasses if she takes advantage of the ½ price deal on a second pair?

_____

Brenda was quite satisfied when her eyeglass order arrived. However, she did not like the cases that came with the glasses, since they were just soft vinyl, slipcover-style cases. Brenda prefers a hard case that will give the glasses a bit more protection from being dropped or accidentally sat on.

Brenda has selected a brown leather hard-cover case at a cost of $29.99, and for her second pair of glasses a hard plastic case that costs $6. She also bought a special anti-fog glass cleaner in a small spray bottle for $2.39. Sales tax on these purchases is 8%. If Brenda pays with a $50 bill, how much money should she get back in change? _____

Election Data Worth Noting

Paula has been closely following the election races in the area where she lives. There are a number of local political offices being contested. This year, Paula has made a special effort to learn the issues involved in each race. She wants to be well informed about all the candidates before she casts her vote.

After the elections were held, Paula was surprised to see in the local newspaper that only 3,110 people in her county actually voted. The local supervisor of elections reported that the total number of people in the county registered to vote was 7,775. The light voter turnout was blamed on a combination of voter apathy and poor weather conditions present on election day. What percentage of total registered voters cast votes in Paula's county on election day? _____

THANKS FOR YOUR VOTE!

Paula was especially interested in one of the local school-board races. Mr. Browne, a retired teacher with a good reputation, was running against an incumbent on the school board, Mrs. Smith. Mrs. Smith had been very critical of the school board during the time she served and was often outspoken at board meetings.

In this particular race, Browne received 880 votes to Smith's 220 votes. Paula thinks that voters were turned off by Mrs. Smith's negative comments about other school-board members and her frequently noisy behavior at board meetings. What percentage of the total vote did Browne receive? _____

Carpenter Cuts It Close

Jesse works as a carpenter, mostly building decks and other outdoor structures. He is always looking for ways to conserve materials, especially wood. This makes for good business, especially since wood is the most expensive consumable item Jesse uses at job sites.

Before making a cut, Jesse always measures each piece of wood and double-checks the measurement against his plans. This reduces the number of mistakes made and ensures that waste will be kept to a minimum. Jesse is currently working on a project for which he needs 3 pieces of wood cut from a single board. The board he will use is 12 feet, 1 inch in length. Jesse must measure carefully, since he wants to cut the length of the board at intervals that will leave 3 equal pieces. Each time the board is cut, ⅛ of an inch of wood length is lost due to the saw cut. How long will each piece of wood be when the cuts are finished? _____

Jesse does not always work exclusively in wood. For a piece of playground equipment he is building, Jesse will need to cut thick pieces of nylon rope and weave them into a platform. He will then secure this rope platform into a wooden frame and install it on the piece of playground equipment. Jesse has purchased a piece of nylon rope 50 feet in length. He needs to get 6 equal pieces from this length of rope. Ordinarily, the cut ends of a piece of nylon rope must be melted to prevent fraying. Melting the rope causes ⅜ of an inch to be lost. For this project Jesse will attach the rope securely inside a wooden frame and the melts are unnecessary. How long will each piece of rope be? _____

MEASURE TWICE, CUT ONCE!

More About Jesse's Carpentry Projects

Jesse purchased a piece of oak plywood with dimensions of 4 feet by 8 feet. Part of this board will be used to make doors for a cabinetry project, and the remainder will be saved for future use. This piece of oak plywood cost $45.99, and Jesse will be careful making his cuts so that no mistakes are made. Two cabinet doors, each with dimensions of 2 feet by 3 feet will be cut from this piece of plywood. Not counting the wood lost to the saw blade when the cuts are made, how many square feet of the original oak plywood will be left after the rough cabinet doors are cut out?

_____

Jesse purchased a stack of fine walnut boards from somebody who was cleaning out a workshop and closing up business. Jesse paid $295 for the lot, more than he is used to paying for the type of wood he normally works with. The walnut boards had been carefully stored for a number of years and were in excellent condition, so Jesse was willing to take a bit of risk in buying them.

WHAT A GREAT DEAL!

Back at his workshop, Jesse inspected the wood and began considering possible uses for it. After giving much thought to the matter, Jesse decided that the walnut was far too nice for the types of projects he is normally asked to build. Jesse called the owner of a shop that specializes in the repair and restoration of antique furniture. The owner agreed to drop by Jesse's workshop and take a look at the wood. Jesse was hoping to recover his own cost in the wood, but he was pleasantly surprised to be offered $420 for the walnut boards. How much profit will Jesse make on the walnut boards if he accepts this offer? _____

95

Hiker Takes Time

Earl likes spending time outdoors. Hiking is his favorite outdoor activity. Earl travels to nearby national parks to do most of his hiking. He keeps a journal of his hiking experiences so he can remember where he has gone, what trails turned out well, interesting events, and any other information he chooses to record.

Earl has been studying his hiking journal. He noticed that his favorite mountain trail takes him about the same amount of time to cover nearly every time he goes. The trail is described in park literature as being "four miles over challenging terrain." Earl has hiked this trail four times. The first time he completed the hike in exactly 3 hours. The second time it took 3 hours, 18 minutes, since the weather was rainy and trail conditions were sloppy. The third time Earl hiked this trail was his fastest trip, 2 hours, 48 minutes. Earl's most recent hike along this trail took 2 hours, 50 minutes. Earl began his calculations by adding all the hiking times together and dividing by the total number of miles walked during his four hikes along this trail. What is the average amount of time it takes him to cover 1 mile of his favorite mountain trail? _____

Earl has worn out a number of pairs of hiking shoes pursuing his hobby. He likes to buy his hiking footwear only from stores that offer a money-back guarantee. Occasionally, Earl will have to return a boot or shoe after having tried it out on a trail. Sometimes it is not the fit, but poor workmanship that causes a shoe to be returned for a refund. In the past year Earl has had to return two pairs of hiking boots for various reasons. One pair cost $79.99 and wore blisters on his feet. The other pair cost $119.59, and part of the sole came unglued. How much money did Earl avoid losing by having the ability to return these boots? _____

IF THE SHOE FITS...

More About Earl's Hiking

Earl purchased a copy of the newest edition of a popular hiking guidebook. He has been reading this guide and looking for hikes that sound interesting. Earl thinks that he has found a few. The first is an 8.6-mile hike along the base of a mountain. It links with another trail that is 3.7 miles along a river. The river trail plays out just at the beginning of a 5.5-mile hike that passes near an abandoned mining camp and eventually leads back to the main highway.

Earl is thinking to combine these trails into one long hike. He probably will camp overnight at some point along the river trail hike. A friend can drop him off by car at the starting point and pick him up later along the highway. How long is the route Earl has mapped out for this hike? _____

LET'S TALK HIKING!

Earl has been asked to teach a course called Hiking Basics to a youth group associated with a local civic club. He is really looking forward to talking about his favorite hobby and sharing some of his favorite hiking stories. Earl will meet with this class four times, for a one-hour session each time. He has been offered a total of $180 to teach these classes. Earl knows that he will have to spend another 20 minutes preparing materials for teaching each of the one-hour class sessions. How much total time will Earl spend in teaching and preparing for all the Hiking Basics classes? _____

Competitions Lure Pet Enthusiast

Meyer has seen several different programs on television on which people take their pets to compete in events. Meyer's dog is not traditional show material, but the terrier has a knack for getting through tight spots very quickly. Meyer thinks his dog, Scampy, would do well in an obstacle course event of some kind.

Meyer set up a makeshift obstacle course in his backyard to give Scampy practice. He used lawn furniture, sheets, and other household items as obstacles. He showed Scampy the course and led him through it the first time. Scampy then tried the course while being timed by Meyer and took 1 minute, 5 seconds to finish. Meyer kept working with Scampy over the next few days and was impressed with how fast the dog was able to learn the obstacle course. Scampy took only 22 seconds the next time Meyer timed him. How much time had Scampy shaved off his first time trial on the obstacle course? _____

Meyer wrote to one of the programs for an information packet on how to enter Scampy. He was disappointed to find out that the program had all the contestants it needed for this season's remaining shows. He was invited to submit a video of Scampy for next season's programming, to begin in six months.

Meyer decided that he would work with Scampy every day for at least an hour, with his goal being 40 hours of training per month. If Meyer meets his monthly training goal with Scampy, how many hours of training will the dog have had by the time the program begins accepting applications again? _____

Carnival Attendant Seeks Opportunities

Bucky is an experienced carnival attendant. He has worked many of the finer carnival circuits in the Midwest. Bucky ran the ring-toss game for a number of years in Gypsy Jules' Carnival. He also worked as a weight-guesser with the widely acclaimed Little Bit of Rumania Carnival. Bucky's specialty was acting as announcer for the Mysterious Tattooed Wild-man of Nepal. Bucky was surprised to find that this wide range of experience was not much help in finding a job when he recently moved to Florida.

Bucky has decided to use his savings to buy a business. He is purchasing the Alligator and Dangerous Snake Ranch. The ranch is located several miles outside a beach resort city along Florida's northwest coast. It is near an interstate exit and draws most of its customers from a series of billboards situated along this interstate route. Business has declined for the Alligator and Dangerous Snake Ranch in recent years because most tourists find this sort of contrived exhibit to be both boring and pointless. But Bucky is confident that he will make a success of the business. He has agreed to make monthly payments to the former owner over a 10-year period in order to pay for the ranch. For the first five years, Bucky will make payments of $275 monthly. During the last five years, his monthly payment will drop to $175. Including Bucky's $24,000 down payment, how much money will he have paid for the Alligator and Dangerous Snake Ranch once it is fully paid for? _____

IT'S SNAKE TIME!

Bucky has decided to sell the ranch's collection of stuffed exhibits. Those exhibits are too dull for the new image Bucky is trying to create for the ranch. He wants to turn the Alligator and Dangerous Snake Ranch into an exciting tourist destination with only live animal exhibits. Bucky expects the stuffed exhibits to bring a total of $3,250 once all of them have been sold. With the money, he will first buy two parrots at a cost of $975 each to use with his Dead Pirates of the Caribbean display. He will use the remainder of the money toward the purchase of a rare albino alligator that costs $5,000. How much more money will Bucky need to scrape up in order to complete the alligator purchase? _____

Sewing Shop Goes Upscale

Millie owns Neat Notions Sewing Shop. Most of the shop's business is built around alterations and custom sewing work. Millie also takes in a fair number of orders for hand-tailored uniforms, evening dresses, and swimwear. Lately, she has been considering a number of changes for her business.

One thing Millie wants to change about the business is the retail portion of Neat Notions Sewing Shop. She sells material, patterns, and other sewing items in one corner of the shop. That portion of the store generated only $12,896 in profits last year. It also attracts a number of bored women with nothing else to do who come in to drink coffee all day while they look through pattern books. Millie plans to eliminate that portion of the shop and move in a few more sewing tables for her staff. Millie thinks that she could easily increase her alterations business, and after a time it would more than make up for the lost profits from the retail shop. On average how much profit per week does the newly expanded alterations side of the business need to make up to recoup the lost retail profits? _____

Millie has just ordered a whole new assortment of fine fabrics to use for her small line of evening dresses. She has been encouraged by the increase in other areas of the business since the retail portion of the shop closed. It seems that more people are coming into the shop every day to place custom orders.

BUSINESS IS SEW-SEW!

In figuring a customer's bill, Millie charges $16 per hour for sewing a custom design. She then adds the charge for materials. One evening dress she recently finished cost the customer $180. If materials for this dress were billed at $84, how many hours of labor went into making the dress?

_____

More About Millie's Sewing Shop

Millie has been talking with Mr. Lee of Lee's Custom Suits. She has known him for a long time through a local business club. In past years they have referred customers to each other based on their own special areas of work. In talking with Lee, Millie found that he was planning to move his business to a new location. Millie thinks that he might be the ideal partner for her shop, since he would bring in a totally new area of business. Expenses for each of them would also be reduced under such an arrangement. Lee is interested in the idea but concerned about the finances involved.

Millie and Mr. Lee have agreed to share equally the cost of having their attorneys and accountants sit down together to study the matter. Millie's attorney charged $225 to study the idea, while her accountant charged only $90. Mr Lee's attorney charged $180 and his accountant's bill was $125. The idea of a partnership turned out to be unworkable due to the tax implications. How much money does each of them owe to the team of accountants and attorneys? _____

A number of people have stopped in Neat Notions Sewing Shop to ask if the business can produce hats, scarves, belts, and other custom accessories. Millie has had to turn most of this business away, since she has no one on staff to handle it. Millie is thinking of hiring a person to work exclusively on this potential line of accessory merchandise. She even has someone in mind, a designer working for one of her competitors across town.

Millie has had lunch with this particular designer before and learned that she was making $28,000 a year, plus a benefits package valued at $8,500 per year. Millie plans to meet with her again to see if she can be lured away from her present employer. Millie is prepared to match her present compensation package and to also offer her a raise in salary of 15% per year. If hired, how much money per year would the new employee cost Millie? _____

Hours Limited at Service Department

Chester runs the service department at a local automobile dealership. His job is supervising the mechanics, scheduling appointments, and ensuring that the customers are satisfied with the work performed. Chester supervises eight mechanics. Each of the mechanics is expected to work an 8-hour day during the Monday through Friday workweek.

The number of cars Chester can schedule for service during a week is limited by the number of mechanics he has on staff and the total number of work hours those mechanics can put in during that week. For instance, Chester cannot schedule 200 cars, each needing 2 hours of service work, all for the same day. There simply are not enough mechanic hours available. How many total hours of mechanic time are available to Chester for scheduling appointments during a given week? _____

The mechanics supervised by Chester are all paid $16.00 per hour for work performed during a regular 40-hour week. Occasionally, work will pile up at the dealership and Chester has to open up the service department on a Saturday to get things caught up. When Chester requires the mechanics to work overtime, he pays them a special rate of 1.5 times their normal rate of pay, commonly called "time and a half." What does Chester pay the mechanics per hour on Saturday whenever they are required to work overtime?

_____

More About Chester's Work at the Dealership

Chester is not only responsible for running the service department at the dealership, but also for arranging continued training for the mechanics in his department. Chester decides which mechanics need to attend company workshops in order to gain additional expertise in a particular area of automobile maintenance or repair.

Chester is sending two mechanics to a company-sponsored workshop in a distant city. The two will be gone for three days attending a workshop on the safe handling and proper disposal of hazardous waste materials. This is an area of special interest to the dealership's owners, as they have previously been fined for improper storage of used oil. Chester was told that it would be his responsibility to solve this problem. The two mechanics involved will not be available to put in their normal 8-hour workdays while they are attending the workshop. How many lost mechanic hours will their absence create for Chester's appointment scheduling? _____

Chester has been asked to explain a customer's bill. The customer wants to know why he has been charged for 11.5 hours of labor when the shop only had his car for a total of 6 hours! Chester politely explained that two mechanics each worked on his car for 5.75 hours to complete the job in time for the car to be ready for pick-up at closing time. If the customer is billed at $40 per hour for work done on his car, how much is the labor portion of his bill? _____

Fishing Problems Beat Other Kinds

George has his own fishing boat. He believes in the old saying "A bad day fishing is better than a good day at work." George prefers saltwater fishing to freshwater fishing. He likes to take his boat offshore and troll for big-game fish, such as marlin, wahoo, and dorado.

George's fishing trips are often beset by problems, which he really does not mind dealing with. George thinks that problems that have to do with fishing are better than any other kind of problems. On a recent trip George noticed that a taillight on his boat trailer was not working. He stopped by a marine supply store to replace the light and buy a few other items on his list. The taillight turned out to be corroded and the entire fixture had to be replaced at a cost of $12.29. George also bought a pack of emergency flares at a cost of $24.99 and a boxed assortment of electrical fuses for $8.59. He almost forgot to pick up two extra packages of flashlight batteries but was reminded of them by seeing a display near the cash register. The batteries were $4.99 per package. Sales tax on his purchase was 6.5%. George paid with a $100 traveler's check. How much was his total purchase? _____

George encountered another problem on a recent fishing trip. A large fish snapped one of his light-action fishing rods and stripped all the line off the reel. George thought that it was one of the best fights he had ever had with a fish. The line cost $8.79 to replace and the fishing rod cost $65 to replace. George later realized that the gears in the reel had been stripped by the fish and paid $20 to have a technician at a sporting-goods store replace them. Had he known about the gears, he might have just purchased an entirely new outfit for $89.99. How much did the fight with this fish cost George? _____

Would-Be Rancher Loses Small

Terry has an interest in ranching. He has only two acres of land, but Terry is full of ideas for turning it into a profitable ranch. Terry's latest scheme involved raising chinchillas. Friends tried to tell Terry that there was no market for chinchillas since most people no longer wear fur coats. They also warned him about responding to an ad in the back of a magazine. But Terry was convinced that chinchillas were the right way to go, and he ordered 12 of these animals from a dealer halfway across the country.

While Terry was waiting for the chinchillas to arrive, he built a large cage with separate compartments for the animals to live in. Terry began calling this the chinchilla condo. Materials for the condo cost him $329. Terry also bought $36.50 in supplies for the chinchillas from a local feed-and-seed store. He wanted to be ready when the animals arrived. Terry began to get nervous when the chinchillas did not arrive on the date promised. He had already sent the company a check for $49 per animal, plus $14.75 each for shipping. When Terry tried calling the company, he found that the phone number had been disconnected. It looks like his chinchilla scheme will be a total loss. How much money has Terry lost on the idea? _____

Not a person to dwell on setbacks for long, Terry has a new idea. Fishing worms are in great demand in his area, and Terry wants to get a piece of this lucrative business. He has noticed that a nearby bait store sells a pint-sized container of worms for $4.99. Terry thinks that he could raise worms and sell them just by putting up a sign along the road in front of his house. Terry plans to price his worms at $4.19 per pint, undercutting the nearby bait store. If Terry can sell four dozen of these pint containers of worms per month, how much money will he take in? _____

Collector Can't Get Enough Advertising Items

Franklin collects advertising items. His collection includes many different kinds of promotional items, practically anything with a company name or logo on it. Franklin has signs, pens, refrigerator magnets, stationery, bottle openers, matchbooks, T-shirts, and a multitude of other items used by companies to advertise their products.

Franklin's collection is not scattered around his house. It is neatly contained in just two rooms. The collection began in a spare bedroom with dimensions of 12 feet by 14 feet. But the collection quickly grew beyond this bedroom's capacity. Soon Franklin was also putting items in his 40-foot by 24-foot basement. It was not long before the basement was set aside entirely for the purpose of housing Franklin's collection. How many total square feet of floor space does Franklin have set aside for his advertising collection? _____

Franklin just acquired from another collector a dozen pocketknives bearing the advertising logo of a chain-saw company. He paid $100 for the group but does not plan on keeping all of them. Franklin has decided to sell 6 of these pocketknives to other collectors, and he will keep the remaining 6 for his own collection.

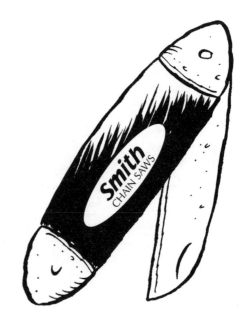

When Franklin met with the collector groups he is involved with, interest in the pocketknives was quite keen. He managed to sell all of the pocketknives he had intended to sell for $12 each. How much money does Franklin now have invested in the remaining pocketknives with the chain saw company logo? _____

More About Franklin's Collection

Franklin has an outdoor advertising sign for a gas station. He paid only $20 for the sign, but he has never been entirely satisfied with it. Franklin keeps it stored in an area of his basement set aside for items he uses as trading material if something comes along worth trading for.

Franklin mentioned his gas station sign at one of his collector meetings, during a time set aside as the swap period. Another collector offered him four milk bottles in trade for the sign. Each bottle had a different dairy's logo embossed on the side. The other collector valued the bottles at $10 each. If Franklin accepts these bottles in trade for his gas station sign, what will his average cost be for each of the bottles? _____

I LIKE COLLECTING DOLLARS THE BEST!

Franklin keeps meticulous records about his collectibles and how the items were acquired. He pays special attention to recording in his log when a particular item was acquired, from whom it was acquired, and the amount paid or items traded for it.

In conducting his yearly inventory, Franklin counted 841 different items in his advertising collection. Franklin's total cost for these items is $1,715.64. A number of items in his collection were free, given to him by companies advertising their products. Several of the more expensive items in Franklin's advertising collection cost over $50 each. What is Franklin's average cost per item for each item in his advertising collection? _____

Proven Approach Works for Cautious Investor

Gwen is a cautious investor. Gwen keeps most of her money in a savings account, but she also has a portfolio of stocks she has chosen carefully over the years. She is proud of her stock investment record, having made money in the stock market for 46 out of the last 50 years. Gwen does not believe in frequently trading stocks or chasing whatever new company stock everyone else is trying to buy. Gwen also thinks that the new online trading frenzy is just a way for people with little experience investing in stocks to lose most of their money! Gwen makes her own investment decisions after consulting with her accountant, banker, and attorney.

Recently, one of Gwen's long-held stocks, Trust Banking Company, was bought by Mammoth Bank. Gwen owns 1,000 shares of Trust Banking Company. Mammoth Bank will pay shareholders of Trust Bank 2.5 shares of Mammoth stock for each share of Trust stock owned. How many shares in Mammoth Bank will Gwen hold once her Trust Bank stock has been converted? _____

Gwen is thinking of selling her shares in Sparkly Soda and Syrup Company. She first bought the stock many years ago, getting 50 shares at a total cost of $1,025. Over the years the stock split several times. (Investors were given additional shares of stock by the company, based on how many shares they already owned.) Gwen never bought any more stock in Sparkly Soda beyond her initial investment. She now owns 300 shares of Sparkly Soda. The stock is currently worth $44 per share. How much profit could Gwen make by selling all her shares of Sparkly Soda and Syrup Company at current prices? _____

BUY LOW-SELL HIGH!

More About Gwen's Investments

Gwen's hairdresser has been recommending stocks to her for a number of years. Gwen seldom pays any attention to the woman, since much of what she says is extraordinarily silly. But recently Gwen's hairdresser told her about a company that Gwen actually found interesting.

BioPharmx is a medical research company developing a number of new drugs for dealing with a wide array of medical problems. After doing some further research, Gwen has decided to invest in BioPharmx. She has $5,000 she plans to use for buying this company's stock. Not including commissions, how many shares of BioPharmx will Gwen be able to buy if its current share price is 75½ per share? _____

Gwen is planning to sell all her shares in Western Exploration Oil Company. She has 700 shares of Western Exploration stock. Gwen thinks that the company is a fine investment, but she wants to use the money from the stock sale to pay for her granddaughter's college tuition.

Shares of Western Exploration are trading at 210¼ on the stock exchange. Gwen thinks that all the shares will sell at this price. Once the sale is completed, she will set aside $100,000 from the sale for her granddaughter's tuition fund. How much money will be left over from the sale of the stock after the tuition fund is set aside? _____

Construction Company Troubleshooter Stays Busy

Craig works for New Beginnings Construction Company. His job title is Special Site Consultant. What this means is that Craig is sent around to different New Beginnings' job sites to troubleshoot problems as they develop. In his job Craig has had to think of some clever ways to solve difficult problems that pop up during the construction process.

Craig has been called out to a factory site where a large water tank is being repaired. The tank is ordinarily used as part of the factory's production process. Its capacity is 12,000 gallons. At present, the tank is only 40% full, but it must be entirely empty in order for the work crew to complete the necessary repairs. The factory pump being used to empty the tank failed, leaving Craig to think of a solution. Craig brought with him four commercial pumps, each capable of removing 24 gallons of water per minute. Once the pumps are all set up and operating, a crew will keep them running continuously until the water is pumped out of the tank. How long will it take for the water still left in the tank to be completely pumped out? _____

New Beginnings Construction Company has experienced a problem with several beach cottages they recently sold to customers. Portions of vinyl flooring material have come unattached in places and curled up where the glue failed to hold. After inspecting the problem at the first cottage, Craig has decided to try a special polymer glue. He has used this glue before on other projects with exceptional results, but there is one drawback. Once mixed, the glue sets up and completely hardens by the time 220 seconds have elapsed. Craig thinks that will be enough time to fix the problem areas. In terms of minutes and seconds, how long does Craig have for making repairs before the glue hardens?

NO SWEAT!

Time Counts at Wood Shop

Jeremy owns a woodworking shop. He employs three people. One of the employees is a wood craftsman with skills nearly as advanced as Jeremy's. Another employee handles all the office work, including answering the telephone. The third employee picks up supplies, runs errands, and handles deliveries. Jeremy has all the normal shop equipment needed for working wood. He also owns a large collection of wood chisels. These wood chisels are used to add a hand-crafted touch to the shop's wood projects.

Jeremy's wood shop is open only during the week, Monday through Friday. Shop hours are 8 a.m. through 4 p.m. Jeremy pays the skilled wood craftsman a salary of $500 per week. He pays the other employees $8 per hour. What is Jeremy's total payroll cost per week? _____

Jeremy and the skilled craftsman have been working together on a complex cabinet project. The two began the job together on Monday morning when the shop opened at 8 a.m. They worked together on this project until closing time at 4 p.m. The two resumed work on the cabinet Tuesday morning when the shop first opened at 8 a.m. At 2 p.m. Jeremy told his craftsman to start on another project they had pending. Jeremy then worked alone on the cabinet, continuing with the project even after the employees had gone home for the day. He finished his decorative carving and then applied a coat of oil finish to the cabinet. Jeremy looked at his watch when the cabinet was finished and was surprised to see that it was 8 p.m.! How many hours went into completing this cabinet project?

_____

Importer Evaluates Stores

Holiday International Imports is a large corporation specializing in decorative items used for celebrating holidays. The store imports a variety of goods from countries around the world, including party favors and food items. Holiday Imports has two types of stores open to the public. It operates huge warehouse stores in both New York City and San Francisco. These two warehouse stores are actually superstores of immense size. Holiday Imports has 18 other retail stores, much smaller in size and mostly located in other coastal cities.

During the course of a year, a warehouse superstore typically does six times the dollar sales volume of one of the regular retail stores. If a warehouse store does $2,670,000 in sales during a given year, how much should one of the retail stores make in sales in a year? _____

Holiday International Imports has had an amazingly good year for sales. Profits are up substantially. The board of directors has taken $2,100,000 and set it aside to share with the dedicated employees that made the year so good for the company. The board plans to give $1,850,400 of the money to the company's president. He wants the bonus to buy a vacation cottage in Martha's Vineyard. The rest of the money will be equally split among the 1,200 other company employees. How much will each of the other employees receive as a bonus for his or her contributions to the company's successful year? _____

SHOW ME THE MONEY!

More About Holiday International Imports

Holiday Imports has arranged to purchase 1,200,000 flags from a distributor of manufactured goods in China. The bulk of this order is made up of American flags that will be sold prior to the Independence Day holiday. The rest of the shipment is made up of flags representing other places, such as Ireland for St. Patrick's Day celebrations, etc. The total shipment of flags cost Holiday Imports only $18,000.

When the flag shipment arrived at the San Francisco store, it was discovered that all the American flags had been printed with the field of stars on the wrong side. The rest of the flags appeared to be useable. The company buyer at Holiday Imports was quite discouraged to discover that the distributor who sold these flags to them was out of business and could not be located for a refund. If the misprinted American flags numbered 760,000, how many flags can still be sold from this shipment? _____

Holiday International Imports is buying the Imported Goodies Company. Imported Goodies carries merchandise very similar to that sold by Holiday Imports. The merger makes sense because Imported Goodies is a successful chain with 12 stores located in areas not covered by Holiday Imports.

Holiday Imports will pay $22,320,000 to the shareholders of the Imported Goodies Company. Holiday Imports has also agreed to assume debts of the Imported Goodies company amounting to $855,900. How much money will it cost Holiday International Imports to fully acquire the Imported Goodies Company? _____

Perfect Picture Framing

Sandra is using her vacation time to catch up on a number of household chores. She will also do some hobby-related projects she has been wanting to take care of for a long time. One of the things Sandra will do is reframe some pictures, cutting new mats where needed and making the frames herself.

Sandra has a large oil painting of a landscape scene that she plans to put into a new frame. The old frame is just too dark for this painting. Sandra wants the new frame to be lighter in color and narrower than the old frame. The painting measures 30 inches by 44 inches. The frame she is planning to make will extend 2 inches around the painting on all sides. How many square inches of wall space will the newly framed painting take up when Sandra is finished with it? _____

Sandra has a large piece of mat board 36 inches by 48 inches. She plans to cut this mat board for a project. She needs a piece of this mat board cut in the shape of a rectangle. The piece to be cut must have dimensions of 1 foot by 2 feet. Sandra is planning to cut this piece out of a corner of the large mat board. (This will make for the most efficient use of the larger piece.) How many square inches of mat board will be left of the larger piece once the 1 foot by 2 foot piece has been cut out?

_____

More About Sandra's Framing Projects

Sandra has been thinking of buying a large table to use for crafts and hobbies. The table will need a durable finish and lots of surface area for spreading out materials. Sandra has a spare room where such a table could be set up. The room is empty right now, with dimensions of 12 feet by 14 feet.

Sandra has narrowed her choices to a hobby table that is 3 feet wide by 6 feet long. The table meets all of her requirements. It is sturdy, with plenty of surface area. The table is actually a cabinet as well. It has drawers and shelves underneath the table surface for storing hobby supplies and materials. If Sandra buys this table and moves it into her spare room, how many square feet of floor space will be left available for other things? _____

IT'S ALL ABOUT HOBBIES!

Sandra purchased a poster she likes. The poster is really not worth putting into an expensive frame. Sandra is planning to just cut a piece of mat board for the poster, and then she will put it on the wall as is. The poster is 20 inches by 36 inches. The mat board will cover only a 1-inch border portion all the way around the poster. (This is necessary so that the poster can be taped to the mat board on the side not normally seen.) How many square inches of the poster will be visible once the mat board has been placed over the poster?

_____

Hospital Makes Patient Sick

Mr. Green was admitted to St. Helena Medical Center after having a minor heart attack. He is feeling much better but is anxious to leave the hospital. Mr. Green does not trust hospitals and thinks that everything they have to offer is way too expensive. The nurses treating him are also anxious for Mr. Green to leave the hospital because he is driving them all crazy with financial questions.

Every time a meal is delivered or medicine administered, Mr. Green insists on knowing the cost. He will not allow a test or any kind of treatment until he has been advised how much he is being charged for the procedure. Mr. Green keeps a notebook by his bed recording all the costs he has encountered. So far, his five-day stay at St. Helena Medical Center has cost him $4,275. If his daily expenses continue to average the same amount, how much will Mr. Green have spent after seven days in the hospital?

_____

Mr. Green has met with his insurer. He was relieved to discover that all of the expenses he incurred while in the hospital were completely covered by his medical policy. The next time he is hospitalized, he will try to relax and enjoy himself instead of worrying about money! Mr. Green pays $212 per month for his medical insurance. Since his recent hospitalization, he has come to think that the premiums he pays are monies well spent. How much does Mr. Green's health insurance cost him per year? _____

Fat Fish Make for Good Business

Marge and Tim own the North Waters Fishing Preserve. The preserve is essentially a private fishing lake stocked with trout. Marge runs the office and handles the fish management side of the business. Tim guides the customers and sees that their trips are enjoyable. Marge and Tim also run a small guest lodge by the lake with four rooms. The rooms tend to stay fully booked during the busy fishing season.

Marge has purchased 800 trout fingerlings from a hatchery. When the fish arrive, they will be kept in holding ponds and fed with pellet food until they are large enough to be released into the main lake. The trout will be fed carefully measured amounts during the four weeks they are in the holding ponds. One pound of food will feed eight trout for two weeks. How much fish food will Marge need to order to meet the needs of the trout during the time they are confined to the holding ponds?

_____

Tim is meeting four clients at the airport and taking them all to dinner. He will then check them into the lodge's four rooms. The four work for the same company and are celebrating a recent business deal by taking this short fishing trip. The clients want an early start on the fishing day since they will be staying at the lodge only two nights. If lodge rooms rent for $84 per night, what will this group owe for their stay? _____

Shipping Company Looks to Improve Fleet

The White Star Shipping Company operates a fleet of 20 ships. The company's principal source of income is transporting cargo for agricultural producers. "We'll get your mangoes to market!" is an old company slogan demonstrating White Star's commitment to its somewhat narrow business focus. White Star Shipping Company still makes it plain that it is devoted to the interests of agricultural shippers.

The White Star Shipping Company has taken two million dollars of last year's profits and earmarked it to use for improving its fleet. The company wants to increase the capacity of refrigerated compartments on each of its ships. This will be advertised to agricultural shippers as another way the White Star Shipping Company is dedicated to serving its agricultural customers. How much money will each ship have for improvements if the money is distributed equally? _____

Many of White Star's ships also have a limited number of modest cabins available for passengers wishing to travel "no frills." The cabins are obviously not White Star's main business interest, but they do produce income for the company. There are 420 passenger cabins among the ships in their line which offer passenger travel. Those cabins generated a total of $512,400 last year. Total expenses associated with operating the passenger cabins were $50,400. On average, how much did each cabin earn in profit last year for White Star Shipping Company? _____

BON VOYAGE!

More About White Star Shipping Company

White Star Shipping Company has suffered a large setback. The company president even characterized it as "a disaster not seen since the terrible tragedy of 1932." (The terrible tragedy of 1932 involved a 2-ton crate of bananas which broke loose and squashed the company's original founder.) This current disaster refers to the loss of their best cargo ship, the *Margo Mango*.

The *Margo Mango* was a 277-foot vessel and represented the pride of White Star's fleet. Unfortunately, the crew on duty thought they had the night off. So they took the night off to play poker. As a result, the unattended ship slipped its mooring and floated away from the pier. It was found the next day, sunk next to a coral reef. The ship will cost White Star $3,330,000 to replace. The insurance company will pay only $2,500,000 toward the replacement cost, since the crew was negligent. White Star must also pay its own shipping customer $286,500 for the crop of lemons which was lost in the accident. Between the balance not paid by insurance and the amount due the shipper, how much money will White Star Shipping Company end up losing as a result of this accident? _____

SORRY.

White Star has taken on a new contract to transport coffee beans for a customer in Central America. (This new customer has never heard about the negligent crew losing the lemon cargo.) The new customer is paying $101,000 to have its coffee crop transported from a port close to its plantation to the coffee wholesaler in Europe. If White Star charged this customer $2,500 for loading the cargo and 50 cents per pound to transport the cargo, how many pounds of coffee are being shipped? _____

Euro Video Store

The Euro Video Store carries foreign films and small-budget, independent films. This is the niche the store has chosen to specialize in. It stocks very few mainstream films or large-budget, general-release pictures. Customers renting films may keep them for five days with the day of rental counting as the first day. Customers are required to return films on the fifth day. This policy allows customers to watch the film at their leisure, having the opportunity to see it more than once (if it is any good) before returning it. How many times is it possible for Euro Video Store to rent the same tape in the span of a 30-day month, assuming that the tape is returned on schedule and rented again the same day? _____

Euro Video Store is running a sale on video rentals. The manager had signs made to advertise the event, but a mistake was made when the signs were printed. It is too late to send the signs back to be redone, so the manager is trying to figure out a way they can possibly still be used. He must first figure the difference in costs to the customer for each scenario. The signs say "Four video rentals for the price of three." They should have said "Three video rentals for the price of two." It ordinarily costs $2 to rent a video at Euro Video Store. If the signs are used as they now read, how much more will the customer be spending over what the manager originally intended for the sale?

_____

More About Euro Video Store

Euro Video Store is making room for the new DVD format discs. The store is selling out all of its old large-format laser discs. The laser discs will be "blow-out" priced at $2 each. The manager is certain that all the laser discs will be sold at this price. The store will cut back a bit on its videos as well. The manager has sorted videos in preparation for this sale, pulling a number of slow-renting titles. The excess videos will be sold for $1 each, once again a price that will ensure that all are sold. Euro Video Store has 216 laser discs and 199 video tapes earmarked for the clearance sale. How much money will the clearance sale generate once all the tapes and discs are sold?

_____

SELL 'EM!

Euro Video Store has been accumulating movie posters for a number of years. The posters are sent by film distributors to promote a particular movie title. The posters are always sent at no cost to Euro Video Store. The manager of Euro Video counted 184 of these posters on a table in the storage room. Another 74 posters are in a rack in the office. Eighteen posters are currently displayed on the walls. The manager has decided to put all the posters up for sale for $4 each. Store employees were invited to take home their favorite posters as a gift before the sale begins. The employees took home 27 posters. How much money will be made by Euro Video from the posters if all the remaining ones are sold? _____

Charity Struggles for Funds

Beatrice runs a shelter for unwanted parrots. She accepts parrots from owners who no longer want the birds. Many of the parrots that Beatrice accepts come to the shelter with bad habits, such as biting or making loud noises. Some of the birds have also been taught to use offensive language. Beatrice accepts all the parrots free of charge, and she tries to rehabilitate the birds so that they will someday make suitable pets.

Running the shelter is an expensive endeavor. Beatrice must raise $1,350 per month just to meet the shelter's regular expenses, such as food for the birds, rent, and utility bills. On average, the shelter spends another $475 per month for nonrecurring and unexpected expenses. Emergency vet visits, building repairs, and travel expenses fall into this category. Since the shelter's staff is all volunteers, no money is budgeted for salaries. How much money should Beatrice expect the shelter will need in operating funds for a full year? _____

Beatrice has just taken in a parrot. This particular parrot, Louie, is well known to her. He is an Amazon parrot who has been through eight different owners over a period of only seven months. Each time he is adopted out to a new owner, Louie is returned to the shelter soon afterward. During that seven-month period Louie spent only four weeks at the shelter between adoptions. Some of the comments his previous owners have made about Louie include "bites a lot," "spiteful," "won't follow any rules," "very sneaky," "uses vulgar language," and "very cunning for a bird." One former owner even referred to Louie as "an evil little creature." Beatrice is beginning to think that Louie is purposefully spoiling his new relationships so that he will be returned to the shelter. On average, how many weeks did Louie spend with each of the owners involved? _____

Internet Fan Watches Less Television

Dean has always been an avid fan of television. Since he was very young, his family has maintained a cable television subscription. When Dean was in the 7th grade, he took part in a study being conducted by his school counselor. Dean kept a log of all his television viewing during the time the study was being conducted. As a result of the study, it was determined that Dean spent an average of 43 hours per week watching television over a two-month period.

When Dean's family recently bought a computer, he discovered the Internet. Just to satisfy his curiosity, Dean began keeping a log on his own. In the log he carefully recorded all the time he spent watching television and surfing the Net. In the first week of his experiment, Dean found that he had spent 36 hours watching television and 19 hours surfing the Net. During the second week his television time was 35 hours and his Internet time was 20 hours. How much time has Dean spent watching television during this two-week period? _____

Dean was greatly surprised and a little bit shocked by a recent visit to his doctor's office. The doctor warned Dean that he must lose 50 pounds and start getting some daily exercise, or he risks having a heart attack before he is old enough to vote. The doctor has prescribed a diet and exercise plan for Dean which will enable him to loose 1¼ pounds per week. The new diet forbids potato chips, cookies, cakes, and a variety of other unhealthy foods which Dean likes to eat while watching television. Dean realizes that the diet and exercise plan will mean less television and Internet time but figures he must make the changes since his health is involved. If Dean can stick with the program, how many weeks will it take him to lose the recommended 50 pounds?

_____

Answer Key

Horse Buyer Does Homework   page 5
Problem 1: $1,140
Problem 2: $330.00

Old House Needs Fixing   page 6
Problem 1: $1,450
Problem 2: $38.97

More About Mandy and Corner Store   page 7
Problem 1: 12 hrs., 52 min.
Problem 2: 16 sq. yds.

Time Bothers Debater   page 8
Problem 1: 54 seconds
Problem 2: 72 points

Weather Project   page 9
Problem 1: 120 readings
Problem 2: 74 degrees

Planning Goes into Photo Album   page 10
Problem 1: $17.57
Problem 2: $484.00

More About Charlotte and Her Photography   page 11
Problem 1: $.57
Problem 2: $25.83

Boat Show No Bargain   page 12
Problem 1: $28.50
Problem 2: $369.90

More About the Boat Show   page 13
Problem 1: $7,668.00
Problem 2: $73.00

Airplane Not Unlike Automobile   page 14
Problem 1: 54.75 hrs
Problem 2: 350 miles

Art Museum Provides Inspiration   page 15
Problem 1: 1,650 gallons
Problem 2: $15.30

Miles Per Gallon Mean Money   page 16
Problem 1: 17.75 mpg
Problem 2: $2,480.00

More About Annie's MPG Study   page 17
Problem 1: $9.54
Problem 2: 1.75 miles

Curious Student Discovers Old Measurement Units   page 18
Problem 1: 32 gills
Problem 2: 4 pecks

More About Trevor and His Study of Measurements   page 19
Problem 1: 2 ft.
Problem 2: $281.88

Difficult Time for Shampoo Inventors   page 20
Problem 1: $158.48
Problem 2: $21.42

Dog Shopper Weighs Differences   page 21
Problem 1: 5 lbs, 8 oz.
Problem 2: 63 lbs

"Horse Moving Is Our Business"   page 22
Problem 1: $4,650.00
Problem 2: $.45

More About Interstate Horse Transport Company   page 23
Problem 1: $52.31
Problem 2: $53,459.00

Grocery Manager Does the Math   page 24
Problem 1: 60 cu. ft.
Problem 2: $1.70

More About Pete the Grocery Manager   page 25
Problem 1: $1,158
Problem 2: $46,020

Fishing Tournament Makes Big Splash   page 26
Problem 1: $107.02
Problem 2: 11 oz

Computer User Studies Printer Costs   page 27
Problem 1: 3 min
Problem 2: $19.00

Advertising Firm Scrambles to Keep Up   page 28
Problem 1: $400.00
Problem 2: $365,025